Praise for Lee Martin's *From Our House*

"Martin has written a memoir to read slowly and savor. . . . Over the course of the memoir, Martin shows how he and his father learn to overcome their shame and control their rage. The honest and straightforward description of their relationship and their obvious affection for each other completely involve the reader. Highly recommended."—*Library Journal*

"Martin's memoir evokes the secrecy of family violence and the isolation of growing up in a rural community. . . . This is a touching and honest portrayal of family life, violence, disappointment, and coming of age."—*Booklist*

"A lyrical, finely wrought memoir of grief, pain, and joy."—*Chicago Tribune*

"Wise and healing."—*Publishers Weekly*

Praise for Lee Martin's *Turning Bones*

"*Turning Bones* is part memoir, part epic, and part historical fiction. Lee Martin weaves creative technique, research, and personal essay together beautifully, shedding light on history and teaching the reader something new about not only America's maturation, but about modern life as well."—*Mid-American Review*

"A lyrical, imaginative work. . . . This ambitious work weaves together many strong, intriguing people, brought together by a skillful writer for a family reunion across time."—*Publishers Weekly*

"A moving family history and cultural excavation."—*Virginia Quarterly Review*

"Through white space, Martin guides readers through his tale of his family's past, as well as his own, in a captivating tale of love, heartbreak, and redemption."—*Ohioana Quarterly*

"A beautiful intertwining of memoir and personal historical fiction. In a thoughtful, contemplative way, Martin works like his own private detective to make sense of his family and his place in the larger world."—Mary Swander, author of *Out of This World: A Journey of Healing*

"Martin brings his forebears to life with affection and empathy, brilliantly interweaving their stories with his own, and leaving us with a greater appreciation that our lives are but a series of intersecting tales, ones that, with luck, we add to and continue to tell."—Kathleen Finneran, author of *The Tender Land: A Family Love Story*

"Rarely are story and history so effortlessly and enjoyably entwined. Rarer still is this hybrid fruit of the said intersection. *Turning Bones* is a miraculous and many-splendored invention."—Michael Martone, author of *The Blue Guide to Indiana*

Such a Life

AMERICAN LIVES | *Series editor:* Tobias Wolff

LEE MARTIN

Such a Life

University of Nebraska Press   Lincoln

© 2012 by Lee Martin
Acknowledgments for the use of copyrighted
material appear on page vii, which constitutes
an extension of the copyright page.
Manufactured in the United States of America

Library of Congress Cataloging-in-Publication Data

Martin, Lee, 1955–
Such a life / Lee Martin.
p. cm.
ISBN 978-0-8032-3647-9 (pbk.: alk. paper)
1. Martin, Lee, 1955– —Childhood and youth.
2. Authors, American—Homes and haunts—Illinois.
I. Title.
PS3563.A724927Z46 2012
813'.54—dc23
[B]   2011026893

Set in Adobe Garamond.

Contents

Acknowledgments

Many thanks to the following journals, where these essays first appeared or are forthcoming: "Never Thirteen" and "Somniloquy" (*Mid-American Review*); "Drunk Man" (*Arts & Letters: Journal of Contemporary Culture*); "You Want It?" (*Midsouth Review: A Journal of Creative Nonfiction*); "Twan't Much" (*Brevity: A Journal of Concise Literary Nonfiction*); "Who Causes This Sickness," "The Classified Ad," and "Not At This Address" (*The Sun*); "The Fat Man Skinny," "Such a Life," and "A Backward Spring" (*River Teeth: A Journal of Nonfiction Narrative*); "Take, Eat" (*Sweet: A Literary Confection*); "All Those Fathers That Night" (*Gulf Coast*). "Colander" first appeared in *One Word* (Sarabande Books, 2010); "Election Season" is reprinted from *Living Blue in the Red States*, edited by David Starkey, by permission of the University of Nebraska Press, copyright 2007 by Lee Martin.

Such a Life

Colander

One summer morning the telephone rang in my grandmother's house, and, because she was busy washing dishes at the sink, I ran to answer it. She kept the new dial phone on a library table by her bedroom window, a bedroom off the kitchen in the modest frame house where I'd spent the night. It was 1962, and I was seven years old. Progress had come to our sleepy, backwoods part of southern Illinois in the form of telephones you dialed instead of cranked and seven-digit numbers instead of a series of long rings and shorts. My grandmother had all this before my parents did in our farmhouse just two miles east on the County Line Road.

My grandmother's phone was on a party line, and I loved to sneak into the bedroom when she was occupied with her soap opera—she was faithful to *As the World Turns*—and pick up the receiver and eavesdrop on other people's conversations. "Well, I swan," I heard a woman say one day, and I thought how marvelous it sounded when she said it, her voice nearly breathless with disbelief. "I swan." More splendid than it sounded when my grandmother said it. More wonderful because it came to me over that phone line, a voice without a body, just the pure sound of it.

When the phone rang on that summer morning and I answered it, a woman's voice on the other end of the line said to me, "Lee, tell Grandma to bring her calendar."

It was my Aunt Anna, my mother's sister, and I said all right, I would. I'd tell Grandma that instant. *A calendar*, I may very well have thought to myself. *I swan.*

I ran into the kitchen, and I tugged on my grandmother's apron. "Aunt Anna's on the phone," I said, "and she wants you to bring your calendar. Hurry. Quick."

Grandma whisked a calendar from the nail where it hung next to the crank phone she no longer used. She hurried into the bedroom, where I'd left the receiver lying on the library table. She picked up the receiver and held it to her ear. She said, "Anna, I've got the calendar. What's wrong?"

But there was no answer on the other end of the line, and my grandmother looked at me with suspicion in her narrowed eyes, her bunched-up brow. She laid the receiver into its cradle. How I loved that sleek, black phone with its dial that whirred along so merrily when I put a finger into one of its notches and spun it. "Lee," my grandmother said, "it's not nice to story."

She thought I was fibbing, but I wasn't. Aunt Anna was on the phone. She said, "Tell Grandma to bring her calendar." Now suddenly she wasn't there. Just silence, and I said to my grandmother, "Just ask her when she comes to get us."

Aunt Anna was coming in her car, and she and I and my grandmother were going to my parents' farmhouse, where my mother was canning tomato juice.

"Not me," Aunt Anna said when she arrived and my grandmother asked her whether she'd called. Once again, I was suspect.

"Little boys who tell stories grow long noses," my grandmother said, and I kept quiet, not knowing what to say in my defense.

For the most part I was a shy boy, an only child, but somehow I picked up a knack for performance. Given the right circumstances, I could be a ham. My father was a storyteller, animated and full of pizzazz. My mother, like me, was timid. I remember how she sang hymns in church, her voice so soft, only I, sitting next to her, could hear it.

What a surprise, and I hope a delight, it must have been when she discovered that her son, despite his shyness, enjoyed putting on a show—loved, in fact, the music words could make.

I could do voices, and most of those voices came from television, to which I was hopelessly addicted: Walter Cronkite's "And that's the way it is"; Jackie Gleason's "And away we go"; Red Skelton's "Good night, and may God bless." I could do Fred Flintstone ("Yabba Dabba Doo"), Popeye ("I yam what I yam"), Elmer Fudd ("Ooh, that wascally wabbit"). Sometimes I'd come to the supper table after watching a western on TV in which a hardened cowboy had the fortune of a home-cooked meal, and, when I was finished eating, I'd say to my mother, "Much obliged for the vittles, ma'am." Other times I'd burst out with my best Jimmy Cagney, "You'll never take me alive, coppers." Or I'd throw my arms around our collie's neck and wring the sap out of a line from that week's episode of *Lassie*: "Good girl, Lassie. Oh, Lassie. You've come home."

My mother must have wondered who the heck I was, this boy who otherwise would cling to her skirts in the presence of strangers and hope against hope that no one noticed him or, worse yet, spoke to him or, god forbid, asked him a question that required an answer. I was that boy a good deal of the time. A mommy's boy. Even now, it slices me to say the words, to know the truth of them. But there they are. I was the boy who for a few months during second grade worked himself into such a dither that it was easy to feign illness all for the sake of staying home, close to my mother. My parents took me to the doctor, a gruff man who smoked cigars. He prescribed medication for my condition, a teaspoon of clear liquid each morning. In later years I figured out it was sugar water. He suspected what ailed me was all in my head.

It was in my heart too, this feeling of dread. Really, that's what it was. A fear that sometime while I was at school my mother and father would pack up and leave. In addition to being a farmer, my father was a CIA operative, dispatched in the middle of the night, with a sudden call, to places I could only imagine: Moscow or Buenos Aires or East Berlin. His farming was his cover; nothing about our lives was real, only I didn't know that then. I just knew that sometimes I came home and my father was gone. He stayed gone for days on end, and, when I asked my mother where he was, she simply said, "Traveling."

No, that's a lie. A transparent one at that. You knew it as soon as you read it, didn't you? You see what I mean about who I am? A shifter of words, an actor, a liar. I had friends at school and friends on the farms near to ours, but, like all only children, I spent the bulk of my childhood entertaining myself. I made up stories. I never stopped. But here's the truth. My father was a farmer. He lost both of his hands in a corn picker when I was a year old. All my life I've tried to imagine the moment in the cornfield when his picker clogged and he tried to clear the shucking box without first shutting off the tractor. The rollers in the shucking box, studded with hard rubber fingers, were still spinning, and, as he tried to rake away the corn, they grabbed onto his hand and pulled it in between them. When he tried to use his other hand to free the one that was caught, the rollers pulled it in too. He stood there in the field, waiting for someone to find him, and the rollers mangled his hands so badly that a surgeon would have to amputate them. The rest of his life my father wore prostheses, pincers that he called his "hooks." He'd been an affable man but no more. The accident filled him with rage, and, as I grew, the touch I knew most intimately from him came from the lash of his belt and the cold steel of his artificial hands.

I watched for the signs that he was about to explode, about to take off his belt or reach for a yardstick, and whip me. When his rage filled our home, I shrieked and howled, and that was me, the most genuine me I could be, the one wailing—all lungs and throat and nerves and skin.

But there was also joy. In the midst of my father's terror we found ways to love each other. My family was knotty and difficult to define. Any attempt requires sifting through the layers of our contradictions. I was the shy boy who could cozy up to the spotlight. My father could be the fun-loving rake one moment, dark and brooding the next. And my timid mother, who one night said she was fed up with the both of us and she was going, just going. She didn't know where, and I think she might have if I hadn't stopped her. If I hadn't thrown my arms around her legs and begged her to stay. No performance that, and, even if it had been, it would have been a melodrama at best, a real scenery chomper. "Don't go. Please. I'll be good. Don't go." That's what I said, and I meant every word, as honestly and as urgently as I've ever meant anything my whole life.

Sitting here now, I try to recall my mother's voice, and I can almost manage it, but not quite. You'd think we'd remember forever the way our parents spoke, but it's not really the truth, is it? Their voices, once they're dead, become a stir of air, a tingle on the skin, a thrumming in our chests, a murmur heard, fuzzy with static, on a phone line—you know the sort I mean, that voice from another line bleeding over into the background of your own conversation; you swear you can almost make out what it says.

When I was small, my mother read to me at bedtime. It's the rhythm of her voice I can recall better than the voice itself, a cadence, temperate and soothing, a tempo steady with comfort and care, a pace pulsing with what she believed all her life—what she'd learned from giving herself over to faith—the conviction that on the other side a peace waited for us all. He name was Beulah, an old-fashioned name these days but one that fit her. Beulah, the promised land in John Bunyan's *Pilgrim's Progress*. Beulah, the heavenly Zion. I could hear her name sang at our little country church: *O Beulah Land, Sweet Beulah Land*. When I try to recall her voice now, I think of that church and drowsy summer Sundays when the windows were open and the breeze came in enough to ruffle the tissue-thin pages of New Testaments. That whisper. That was my mother.

But then there was that night she threatened to leave, and that was another sound of her voice, ugly with misery and grief, as when years later she looked down at my father in his casket and said, in a voice quaking and raw, "I don't even have a picture of him." She had that voice too, and that's the one it hurts me most to recall because, if anyone deserved to avoid the bang and truck too common to our family, it was her.

I have to believe, though, she was happy to have us. Once upon a time she was an old-maid schoolteacher at forty-one, still living with her parents, surely imagining that she'd already made her life. She'd go on teaching school, seeing to other women's children. She'd work in my grandparents' general store evenings and

Saturdays, surrounded by people like my father, not knowing that
one evening he'd stay after hours on the pretense of helping her
close up the store. He was thirty-eight, a bachelor farmer taking
care of his ailing mother. I wonder what he said to my mother that
night at the store. Did he make a joke, cut her a shy grin? Did he
look down at his shoes, stuff his hands in his pockets? Or did he
look her straight in the eye, explain to her that he was a man of
a certain age and she was a woman of like years and there they
were, neither one of them with prospects, and wouldn't it make
sense if they tried things out for a while just to see if maybe they
might be able to get on?

Imagine my mother that night on her short walk across the
road to the modest frame house where she lived with my grandparents, taking her time as she moved through the twilight. I don't
know whether this night fell in spring. I don't know whether there
was light at all, but I prefer to think there was what folks used
to call the *gloaming*, that half-light fading fast. I like to imagine
the melancholy call of rain birds, a breeze moving through the
branches of the oak trees, the lush white pom-pom blossoms of a
snowball bush, and my mother memorizing all this so she could
recall it time and time again before she finally said, "I'm in love
with Roy Martin."

I wish I could keep her there on that night and save her from
what's to come, that day in early November 1956 when she gets
the call about my father's accident and the surgeon has to amputate, when she knows that she and my father are moving into
a way of living they never could have seen coming. Twenty-six
more years to navigate, my mother doing for my father the things
he can no longer do himself: shaving, bathing. When he fin-
ishes with the toilet, he whistles for her. A soft, low whistle from

behind a closed door. An embarrassed "I need you," and that's another sound I remember from my childhood.

"Beulah, peel me a grape!" Mae West orders her character's maid in the 1933 movie *I'm No Angel*.

To type the line now saddens me because I relied on my mother to keep me happy just as my father relied on her for his needs. We often treated her as if she were our servant. I was simply lazy. It was easier to ask her to bring me a soft drink while I was watching television than to get up and go into the kitchen and fetch it myself. When my father died and my mother found herself alone in their house, she told me it was the first time all her life that she had no one to take care of. "I don't know what to do with myself," she said.

She used to tell me it wasn't up to us to question the circumstances of our lives. It was our job, instead, to live them as best we could, to trust that God had a plan for each of us, to know that something that looked like a curse could just as easily be a blessing. I have to admit I don't have the same degree of conviction as she did. I lean more toward my father's skepticism. He knew that sometimes the world has plans for us that ask too much. How could he have possibly felt any differently after that day in the cornfield? He was a man about to shut down his tractor and gather up his wife and son and go to his sister and brother-in-law's house for supper. Then he tried to clear the picker's clogged shucking box; his hands got caught between its rollers, and suddenly he was a different man. It could happen that quickly. That's what my father learned, the way a life could divide into before and after.

My mother was an old-maid schoolteacher, and then she was a wife. She was a wife for four years, and then she was a mother. She was a mother a little over a year. Then my father's accident made her his caretaker. Through it all she loved God. All signs point toward this: She prayed to him each night, kneeling as she must have done since she was a little girl, and put her fingers to her lips. In the silence something took place in her spirit that allowed her to keep moving forward, to sift through the facts of her life, to preserve the things that were good and right—I like to think I was one of them, one of the blessings that saved her.

In the garden she kept each summer, she grew all sorts of vegetables: corn, beets, carrots, tomatoes, green beans, cauliflower, broccoli, peas, peppers, squash. Whatever she could put by for the winter, she did—cold-packed, pressure-canned, frozen—even after she lived alone. She was a young woman during the Great Depression, and she'd learned there was always a day coming she couldn't predict, a day of want, perhaps, and it was always good to put a little something by just in case you needed it later.

Then her body betrayed her. She suffered from hypertension and eventually started having small strokes, transient ischemic attacks, TIA's, that began with a tingle in her lip and moved down her left side, leaving her dizzy and listing. Eventually she suffered from dementia and spent the last few months of her life in a nursing home, aphasic, her speech a series of syllables and sounds, none of them cohering. I sat beside her and patted her hand. I told her I loved her, but I'm not sure she heard or understood.

After she moved to the nursing home, I readied her house for sale. I sorted through her belongings, saving for last the jars and jars of food she'd canned. As I handled those cool mason jars and felt their weight, I recalled summer days, my mother's kitchen hot with tomatoes or corn or beans cooking on the stove and canning jars sterilized with boiling water. My mother in her apron and hairnet, beads of sweat dripping from her nose, her cat's-eyes glasses steaming over when she leaned in to fill those jars with whatever she was intent on preserving. I can still hear the steam rising in the pressure canner, the release valve dancing and jiggling. What did I know then of the noise our living makes? The sounds that mark our give-and-take, the ones we sort and press and try to preserve.

I remember this—a moment frozen in an eternal present:

On the day I tell my grandmother to bring her calendar and she later suspects me of telling a lie, we walk into our farmhouse, and my mother says, "Oh, good you brought it."

My grandmother is holding her food mill, that kitchen tool used for grinding and puréeing. A deep metal pan with perforations in the bottom. A broad blade in its center at the end of a hand crank. After the tomatoes cook, my mother will press them through the food mill, turning the crank so the blade can cull out skins and seeds and allow the juice to pass through the perforations, back into the cooking pot so she can boil it again before she pours it into the mason jars. Part sieve, part mill. My mother calls it a colander, and I understand now she was the one on the phone.

As the years go on, she'll take great joy in telling the story of the day I thought she said calendar, but that day in our farmhouse, even though she's laughing because I confused her voice for my aunt's, the laughter finally fades away, and, when it does, I feel peculiar. It's something about the way my mother looks at me, disappointed, and I don't know what to call this thing I feel, so I seal it up inside me, where it waits to be turned and strained: this shame, this longing.

"Didn't you know?" she says, just a hint of hurt in her eyes. I wish I could tell her now, yes, I knew. I always knew. "Mercy," she says. "Didn't you know it was me?"

Never Thirteen

The first girl I kiss is a girl named Beth. It's 1969, and we're thirteen, about to graduate from the eighth grade. It's spring in Oak Forest. Yankee Woods, the forest preserve that sprawls south from 159th Street to Tinley Park and beyond, is green. The snow cover has melted from the grass; winter's bare trees are in full leaf.

In a few weeks my mother and father and I will move back to southern Illinois for good, my mother retiring after thirty-eight years of teaching, the last six in Oak Forest. But now I'm not thinking about any of that because Beth has asked me to walk her home—at least partway, she says. At least as far as Yankee Woods, she says. At least as far as that. That is, she says, if I want to. Do I want to? Boy, howdy!

We've been boyfriend and girlfriend since midwinter—I, a varsity basketball player, she a varsity cheerleader—which means we've sat together in the bleachers, holding hands during the junior varsity games and on dark buses, traveling home from away games, her head laid on my shoulder, my arm around her. She's taught me two ways of holding hands—palm to palm or fingers interlaced—and we've practiced each, our hands inseparable for long periods of time even though they've ached and sweated, neither of us wanting to be the first to break the grasp. We've enjoyed this cuddling, this snuggling, this cooing and wooing.

But we haven't kissed; we haven't been as bold as that. And I haven't walked Beth home; the two of us have never been alone. In a forest preserve. On a path snaking back through the woods. Just the two of us. We've never been thirteen.

This is the year when night after night I wake from wet dreams, and I know from watching a film in health class that this is the time when "A Boy Becomes a Man." Thanks to Arbor Park School District 145 and to a birds and bees chat with my father, I'm no longer sexually ignorant. But I've had nary an erotic thought about Beth. I've delighted in the scent of her perfume—something strong and fruity—the backward slant of her handwriting, the way she signs her notes to me, "Forever Yours," followed by what has become the official signet of couples in our school: an *S* turned on its side, two short lines drawn through its middle.

These are our sweet beginnings, our first leanings toward love.

That afternoon in Yankee Woods we stop on the trail, and there in the grove of trees, there in the dark, cool shade, she asks me whether I've ever kissed a girl, and I'm so thankful for this moment—even now I remember with immense gratitude how she reached out and touched me lightly on my forearm as if to say, It's all right, whoever you are, it's okay—that I can do nothing but tell her the truth, that I am practically without experience; outside of a chaste kiss from my mother, my lips are virgin lips.

"It's not hard," she says, and she steps closer. She gives me a shy smile. Her hair is thick and blonde and cut short, à la Mary Martin as Nellie Forbush in *South Pacific*, and, like Nellie, Beth is kind and spirited, the girl next door and everyone's friend, eager to be swept away by love. I can still see her in her white oxford shirt, her blue culottes, her white sandals, her books cradled in the crook of her left arm. She lifts her chin, tilts her head to the side, and waits for me to take my cue.

But I, alas, am no Ezio Pinza. I'm a shy boy who happens to be a skilled basketball player, and for that reason alone I have the opportunity to be standing in Yankee Woods, a girl like Beth waiting for me to kiss her.

And I can't bring myself to do it.

"Don't you want to?" she says.

"Well, sure," I say. "I guess."

I don't tell her about all the times I've practiced. I've kissed my hand, a mirror, my pillow. And I don't tell her about the time I couldn't stand the curiosity anymore—what would it feel like?— and asked my mother to kiss me, which she had never before, at least to my memory, done. She kissed me on the lips, and I remember that her own were dry and tightly pressed together, and I came away embarrassed, knowing that I had forced her to demonstrate an affection that she felt, I have no doubt, but also one that was uncomfortable for her to display, being the timid, reserved, come-to-love-late-in-life sort that she was. In her dry, rigid kiss I felt her years of living on the outer edges of the world—preparing her students' lessons while other women tucked their children into bed, sitting through *Gone with the Wind*, all four hours of it, alone at the Arcadia Theater while around her young couples held hands in the dark. "There was an intermission," she would say years later, and she would say it proudly, her one claim to romance from those long years of spinsterhood.

I don't want my mother's life to be mine. I don't want to be old, not at thirteen. I don't want to be unkissed.

"What about my nose?" I say to Beth. "Where do I put my nose?"

I'm serious. It's been a big concern of mine since seeing an episode on *The Patty Duke Show* in which Patty and a boy kept bumping noses when they kissed. I'm afraid that Beth will laugh at me, but she doesn't. She explains patiently that she will tip her head to her right, and I will tip mine to my right, and everything will be fine.

"Ready?" she says.

"All right," I tell her.

And it happens. The next thing I know we're kissing, and, unlike the time when my mother kissed me and I came away wondering what the big deal was, I'm fairly well loose-kneed with the absolute thrill of Beth's lips on mine.

When we finish, I ask her whether I did it right. This is how comfortable I feel with her, how safe. This is how much I trust her as my guide through this uncharted territory.

"Relax your lips," she says. "Don't hold them together so tight."

I feel a dagger piercing my heart, an anger constricting my throat. I've failed at this most important, most essential juncture in my life, and I'll be doomed to years of loneliness. People will take one look at me and know the truth; they'll whisper it among themselves: "Doesn't know how to kiss."

But then, before I can move away from her, Beth kisses me again, and, because she catches me off guard—because I have no time to worry about my performance—this kiss is all response, my lips forming themselves to hers. This kiss is soft, warm, unhurried, the kiss I've been needing since the first time my father whipped me with his belt and my mother did nothing to stop him.

It's been our habit as long as I can remember, these whippings. My father is quick to anger, and I'm not exactly blameless. I'm often stubborn, defiant, easily frustrated, full of sass. I'm often too much like him. People will tell me, long after he's dead, that there was a time when he was good-natured and agreeable, and, although there are glimpses of this man as my father ages, for the most part he's brittle and full of temper. I'm clueless to what I now know, the fact that he spent the last twenty-six years of his life trying to relearn who he had been before the farming accident that cost him his hands and changed him forever.

By the time I'm thirteen, I can't remember ever seeing my parents touch with affection. They don't hug, don't kiss. There are no flirtatious caresses or pats as I sometimes witness between my friends' much younger parents. To me my mother and father are old and humdrum. There is nothing sensuous about them, nothing voluptuous. They have no spice, no juice, no ardor or thrill.

Once in winter, I saw a young man in Yankee Woods sitting on top of a picnic table, his face wrapped with bandages, two holes left for his eyes. My father was driving us through on a Sunday, and suddenly there was the young man just sitting there, a mummy in the cold. Now, after Beth kisses me this second time, I'm thinking of that man, how frail and alone he looked, how even then I hoped that he had someone in his life to love him.

"Better," Beth says. "We'll keep practicing." Then she takes my hand, and we walk on through the forest, and I feel blessed, not knowing that she is only the first in a line of girls, the ones that I hope will save me from my father's rage, my mother's meek reserve, and show me how to love.

The Chicagoland forest preserves are where people go when they have something to hide. The police find bodies there; they find women who have been raped and strangled, women with their throats cut or with gunshot wounds to their heads. Each morn-

ing my father buys a *Sun-Times* from Tony's Corner Store, and I
catch glimpses of headlines:

TORSO FOUND

SUBURBAN SLAYING

FOREST PRESERVE MAYHEM

I know there's a nighttime Yankee Woods, perverse and dangerous. I know what men are capable of doing. I was ten the summer
that Richard Speck broke into a student nurses' dormitory and
killed eight young women. I know there's a darker side to those
first sweet kisses that Beth and I share, but for the time being that
side, one driven by lust and greed, is foreign to me. I ask nothing of her, make no demands. Our hands come together on our
walks through Yankee Woods; we stop and kiss. All this is done
without prompting and through mutual consent.

I suppose I should be embarrassed now—how sentimental I
am, going on and on about a first kiss—but I can't manage it.
When I look at that boy and girl kissing in the dark shade, walking out into bright sunlight, I feel a great tenderness for them and
the affection that they share. They will never again be this age,
never again be this innocent. They're still children really, but just
barely, and, because I know now everything they have to lose, I
want them to linger in the cool woods forever, to be always that
age. All the boy wants is to be in this place with this girl, and, if
they end up kissing, that's fine, and, if they don't, that's fine too.
The girl feels completely safe to be alone with him, hidden in
these woods where sometimes horrible things happen to women.

One evening I come home from Yankee Woods and find my
father and mother in the kitchen of our one-bedroom apartment.
My mother is at the stove frying fish sticks for our supper. The
school day done, she's changed into a cotton housedress and taken

off her necklace and clip-on earrings. She's removed her stockings, and her bare calves are spidery with varicose veins. She's fifty-nine years old. She stands with one hand on her hip, a spatula in her other hand, her back already starting to curve into the stoop that will continue to pull her forward into her old age. Our apartment smells of fish; the hot grease pops and splatters.

My father is sitting at the kitchen table, his reading glasses slipped down on his nose, the point of one hook just beginning to unfurl the centerfold of a *Playboy* magazine. For an instant, before he raises his head and sees me, I catch a glimpse of airbrushed flesh—a golden and naked hip, marked only by the white tan line a bikini bottom has left. I've never in my life seen such a sight, and I'm absolutely stunned because I've seen it now in our kitchen where my mother is frying fish and my father is trying to act as if nothing out of the ordinary is happening.

"What's that?" I say, pointing to the magazine, even though I know darned well what it is. My father tries to shield the glossy cover with his arm, but I can see a blonde-haired woman in a football jersey, its hem rising up on her naked legs. It's oddly delicious for me to catch my father peeking at naked women; though he's always been a gruff man, coarse and often vulgar with language, this is the first time that I've seen him demonstrate any sexual curiosity. He's guilty, and he knows it. I've got him with the goods.

He tries to shift the focus of blame to me. "You're late," he says.

But I won't let him off the hook. "It's a *Playboy*," I announce. "You're looking at a *Playboy*."

My mother bangs her spatula against the rim of the frying pan. "He bought it at the Pick 'n Save." Her voice is tight, barely reigning in her disgust. "Honestly. The idea."

Now I'm caught between feeling a wink-wink camaraderie with my father and a miserable embarrassment because this is all happening—this voyeurism—in the company of my mother, a demure woman who must be appalled that her husband would bring this magazine into her home and display it there in her kitchen. Even now it's hard for me to imagine what my father must have been thinking. He knew as well as I how decorous my mother was, a woman in her fifties by the time the sexual revolution hit, a woman who had spent the first forty-one years of her life living at home with her parents. I have a photograph of her as a young woman about to graduate from high school in 1928. She's wearing a simple dress—its blouse long sleeved and loose fitting—adorned with no fur collar, beads, or bows like the dresses of her classmates. She wears no necklace or brooch or lace. Her hair isn't marcelled. In fact, she's wearing a hairnet, its black elastic band visible on her forehead. Her hands are folded in her lap. She tips her head down, her eyes barely meeting the camera's lens. This is the way I think of my mother; this is the girl I imagine she always thought she was—shy and plain. I doubt that she ever believed she was pretty, even though her face had delicately drawn features and her neck was long and slender and her skin was smooth and turned a golden brown in summer.

How demeaned she must feel this evening in our kitchen while my father looks at naked young women. I've just come from one of my sweet walks through Yankee Woods with Beth, and I stand there feeling something I'm unaccustomed to feeling after leaving her—aroused and ashamed. Though I don't know it then, I'm at one of those points beyond which life will be different for me. I can't say it's my father's fault—already my dreams have turned erotic beyond my control—but it's the fact that he brought that *Playboy* into our home that lures me toward the carnal and the lewd. It's there on the table the way the *Sun-Times* might be or the *Farmer's Almanac* that my father always consults before planting his garden. It's right there, and, because I've seen him looking at it, I believe that I have rights to it too. But my mother is frying those fish, and soon we'll all sit around our kitchen table and have to face one another. As much as I want to be able to do that without shame, I'm drawn by something stronger—call it curiosity or lust—and I can't turn away from it. I'm at the end of innocence. This is what happens to boys; they discover the world of the body, and after that they are never the same around women.

"I want to see it," I say to my father.

"You don't have any business with it," he tells me.

"You were looking at it." I move closer to the table. "I want to see it too."

I pick up the magazine, barely able to believe that I'm holding it in my hands. Already I'm moving toward my room. My mother turns from the stove, and her eyes meet mine. I see the hurt in them, the disappointment, the anger.

"You're surely not," she says, and at first I'm not sure whether she's saying this to me or to my father.

I wait for him to erupt in anger. I listen for the sound I know so well: the jangle of his belt buckle as he unfastens it, the whish the belt makes as he pulls it from his trousers' loops. But all I hear is the fish frying and my father's sigh.

"I don't suppose it'll hurt him," he says, and I go to my room and close my door.

The next day, the last day of school, I walk with Beth through Yankee Woods and beyond, all the way to her house. It's not yet noon—school has dismissed early—and everything feels a little strange to me, not only because it's midmorning and we're out of school but also because in a few days my parents and I will be back in southern Illinois, and come fall, instead of returning to Oak

Forest as we have the past six years, we'll stay downstate. What I've known is coming really sinks in on this morning. I clutch Beth's hand more tightly, knowing that our time together is short. Of course, we've already made our promises to write faithfully, and we've said that, when we turn sixteen and have our driver's licenses, we'll make the five-hour trips south or north to see each other. We've pledged our love forever the way kids do when they have no idea of the different people they'll become. By the time we make this walk through Yankee Woods, we carry something new between us—an urgency that we don't quite know how to handle. We know that time is precious, that soon we'll be apart, and all we can do is rely on what we've picked up from movies and television programs about doomed lovers. We speak in clichés: "You're the only one for me." "I love you more than life itself." "I don't care how long we have to wait." Such maudlin, theatrical mewling, and yet I have no doubt that at the time we say these things we're sincere. It's not our fault that we're in a foreign land, desperately trying to learn the language, fumbling for words to say how much we mean to each other.

At Beth's house her mother greets me with reserve. It's the first time we've met, and it's clear that she's suspicious. This is the beginning, she must be thinking, imagining all the boys who will come, intent on defiling her daughter. But this isn't my plan at all. I'm there because soon I'll be far away, and I want every minute with Beth that I can have. Perhaps, too, I sense that I'll need to carry with me the memory of these days: the way the house is so inviting in its midmorning quiet (the refrigerator hums in the kitchen, a breeze lifts the curtain at the window), and downstairs in the walkout basement family room the air is cool, and Beth and I, finally hidden from her mother, hug for a very long time, not saying a word, just holding on, trying to defy time.

Finally, we hear her mother coming down the stairs, and we move apart. I'm stunned by how quickly we do this, how we erase all sign of our bodies meeting. Beth moves to the stereo and puts on a record; I sit on the couch and fold my hands in my lap. Although I've imagined our affections have always been nonsexual, it's clear now that we know to be careful; perhaps we've learned that we have something to protect from the wary eyes of adults, and it's something precious, something the grownups around us once had and then lost. It's that feeling—that head-over-heels, pie-in-the-sky, stars-in-your-eyes, catch-me-I'm falling-in-love feeling—and if it's puppy love so be it. It's still sweet, and at least for the time it's ours. If we're ashamed, it's not because we feel guilty; if anything, we're embarrassed because we don't think our mothers and fathers are worthy of bearing witness to such romance. If they look on us, we'll lose it; they'll steal it away with their hunger, and then how will we ever get it back?

Beth's mother is a tall woman, and, though she isn't heavy, from the way she moves, her body appears to burden her. Maybe she's worn down from spending too many days alone in her house while her children are in school and her husband is at work. I won't claim to know her story. But still I remember her languid droop as she comes down the stairs and the humorless look on her face.

"I just wondered what you were doing," she says.

The Foundations's "Build Me Up Buttercup" is playing on the stereo, and the room fills with the song's roll of drums, its blare of horns, its rollicking keyboard notes. Such an upbeat tune about love gone sour.

"Mother," Beth says with a sigh. She has one hand on her hip, and she cocks her head to the side and stares wide-eyed at her mother, trying to show her, without saying it, how desperately she wants her gone. "We're listening to records," Beth says, and again she sighs.

Mrs. Sims picks up her cue, understanding that she's ventured into territory where she isn't welcome. She starts back up the stairs. Then, when she's halfway up, she stops and turns to look down on us.

"That's a snappy song," she says. "That's something you could dance to."

Her voice is so sad and full of yearning. I imagine now that she may have been wishing that she could linger awhile in the cool basement, listening to the music, looking at her daughter, who, of course, must have been a reminder of a younger version of herself, one she could recall but never quite recover. Perhaps, like Beth, her nickname was "Toots." Perhaps she wrote the name of her boyfriend over and over on the covers of her notebooks and thought she would "just die" if something happened to keep them apart.

Beth lifts the tone arm from the record. A faint crackle dies off in the speakers, and then there is only the electric hum of the turntable as it revolves. She takes my hand—fingers interlaced—and squeezes it more tightly than I can ever remember her doing. She leans over and kisses me on the lips, and I'm horrified because her mother is watching and now what has always been private between Beth and me is on display, performed with an intent I don't have time or experience to understand.

"Come on," she says, and starts leading me to the French doors that open from the walkout basement to the patio.

"Where are you going?" Mrs. Sims calls from the stairs. Her voice has lost its dreamy, melancholic leisure. Her question is snappish and suspicious.

"Outside," Beth calls over her shoulder as she opens the French doors, and we step out into the warm sunlight.

"It's almost lunchtime," Mrs. Sims says. "Beth, do you hear me? Beth, don't go too far."

In the backyard, toward the rear of the lot, a stack of firewood is enough to shield us from view. We sit on the ground, which is still damp from the spring thaw, and Beth raises my arm and drapes it around her shoulder. She snuggles in close, her hand flat on my chest, and lifts her face to me. She's crying, her cheeks damp with tears, and, when we kiss, I can feel how hot her face is, and I can't help but think of all the times my father has left me sobbing, my legs and arms striped from the lashes of his belt.

Suddenly I'm holding Beth as tightly as I can. I close my eyes and rock her. Neither of us speaks. This moment is more profound and heartfelt than anything we've said to each other since we knew I would soon be moving away. We have no words for what we feel, only our bodies pressing together, and, though I have no idea what it means to love a woman, I've never felt as close to anyone as I do in this moment. I imagine now that every embrace I've ever wanted from my father, my mother, myself, is contained in this hug I'm giving Beth. I want us to stay this way for a very long time—sweetly joined and protected, far away from Mrs. Sims and her languor and her resentment and her mourning.

Then I feel something I've never felt in Beth's presence, and I know, from the diagram in "When a Boy Becomes a Man," that my penis is filling with blood and soon, like the penis drawing in the film, I will be erect, flying at full staff, periscope up, ahoy!

I haven't at all anticipated this happening, and I don't know how to feel about it now that it has. Part of me is caught up in the excitement, and part of me is ashamed and wants it to stop. But that's impossible. Something about the closeness of our bodies, and more than that, the fervor of our embrace, foils all my attempts to lower the mainsail and drop anchor. Suddenly, to complicate matters, images from my father's *Playboy* creep into my mind, and to my horror a few drops of semen leak from me. I glance down at my thigh and see the quarter-sized stain on my chinos. I don't want Beth to see this—I don't want to see it now—because I want this moment to be pure and without tarnish, something golden to last me a long time. But it can never be that because there are men like Richard Speck who would have their desire turn perverse and violent. There are men like my father who would leaf through a *Playboy* magazine in the company of my timid, virtuous mother. I don't understand now, anymore than I did then, the fine line between desire and lust. The truth is, the beautiful and the ugly bleed together; the distance between the two is never as wide as we'd like to think. Perhaps there are just men. Period. Even me—sitting there in Beth's backyard, holding her, as close to knowing love as I've ever been, and still ashamed because my body has announced how base my instincts can be.

I hear the French doors open and then Mrs. Sims calling Beth to lunch. Beth breaks away from me and stands, and I have no choice but to do the same. I can barely look at her. I want to hold her again, but I'm afraid that, if I do, she'll feel the dampness on my chinos and then what will she think of me, this shy boy who has walked her home all those afternoons through the forest preserve.

If she notices the stain on my trousers, she doesn't say anything about it, and for that I've always been grateful. She puts her hand on my forearm, the way she did that first time in Yankee Woods when she asked me whether I'd ever kissed a girl.

"I'll write," she says to me in a whisper. "You too."

Then she runs across the yard to the house where her mother waits. When she's inside, I walk away, disappearing into Yankee Woods once more, this time alone.

When I get home, my mother and father are in the bathroom, the door closed, and I know from the way my father says in a quiet voice, "Be careful on my throat," that my mother is shaving him. I can hear the safety razor scraping over his whiskers, the swish of water as my mother rinses the razor, and the clacking sound it makes as she taps it on the edge of the sink.

I stand in the hallway, trying not to make a sound, something about my parents' cooperation captivating me. I'm listening to them; I'm eavesdropping, and suddenly I feel guilty for keeping my presence hidden and unannounced.

One night, a few years earlier, my father caught a man peeping in our window. I had already gone to bed and didn't know anything about what had happened until much later, when I overheard my father and mother talking about that night. I was astonished. I couldn't quite imagine that a strange man had stood at our kitchen window staring in. I wondered what he had found to interest him, to make him stand there in the dark, watching through the archway that led from our kitchen to our living room, my aging parents moving through the light, readying themselves for bed. They slept on a sleeper sofa in the living room. Now I imagine my mother gently lifting the eyeglasses from my father's face, unbuttoning his shirt, helping him slip his arms from the flesh-colored plastic holsters, the hooks screwed into their ends. She would have raised the canvas harness from his shoulders and draped the hooks over a straight-backed chair. She would have unpinned the cotton arm socks from his T-shirt sleeves and rolled the socks down his stumps. I remember how naked those stumps were after being encased all day in their holsters. I remember the white flesh and how it embarrassed me, a sight not meant for my eyes.

Perhaps it was this that kept the Peeping Tom at our window—those naked stumps and the intimacy my mother and father shared, not the intimacy of lovers but a tenderness and familiarity that became theirs because of my father's accident. So maybe it was my mother's delicate movements as she undressed my maimed father that captivated, as it does me now, the voyeur, and made him feel the sensuality that was so privately theirs. I wonder whether they themselves were even aware of it. I had always thought them sexless, without passion, until now when I stand at the window with the Peeping Tom and realize that all along their lovemaking had been present in the gentle way my mother touched my father when she undressed him, when she held a drinking glass so he could take it in his hook, when she shampooed and combed his hair. I remember the way he gave himself over to her ministering, his frequently gruff voice going soft, his arms, which could jerk so often with bluster and fury, relaxing. I can never fully know the accommodations they had to make after my father lost his hands, but I can remember their murmurs behind closed doors—the sound as lulling as the cooing of mourning doves, as soothing as the rill of a brook hidden in a deep woods, a private code between them—and know that all the while I thought them impotent and numb they were making love each day right before my eyes, and I was too blind to see it; I was too busy being young.

Until the afternoon when I stand in the hallway and listen to them in the bathroom.

"Turn your head this way," my mother says, and I know my father is doing as she asks. How can he not? He depends on her for so much, and she gives it without complaint.

"That's it," he says. "Right there."

Then they aren't talking. I listen to the sounds their bodies make as they move: the harness of my father's hooks squeaking as he turns his head and shoulders, my mother's soft-soled shoes sliding over the tile floor, the gentle whisk of her dress as it brushes across my father's twill trousers.

I listen to their dance, and I think about Beth and the way we clung to each other behind the woodpile. Suddenly, in the presence of my parents' gentle and selfless choreography, my future opens, and it terrifies me with its broad expanse of time, its uncertain possibilities. I step into my adult life, wondering how long I'll need to live, how much I'll need to lose, to learn to love like this.

Drunk Man

We picked him up south of town along the blacktop, this man known to be a drunk man, a man someone like my father couldn't leave out there on a sweltering summer day. "It's Odie Moad." He was already slowing down, braking our Ford pickup. "Jesus."

Ahead of us heat vapor shimmered from the asphalt. The sun beat down on the dust-covered weeds in the fencerows—milkweed and foxtail and turkeyfoot grass. The leaves on the sassafras and persimmon saplings curled for want of rain. A haze hung over the cornfields, the stalks tasseling now and spiking the air with pollen. My father pulled our pickup onto the shoulder and lifted his hook from the special spinner knob on the steering wheel that helped him drive. Hot air stopped rushing through our open windows. Above the hum of the idling engine I could hear mourning doves calling somewhere in the distance and the crackle of burnt weeds and grass underfoot as Odie Moad made his way to the passenger side of our truck.

He leaned in through the open window, and I smelled the

whiskey on his breath. The whisker stubble on his chin, silver-flecked in the sunlight, scraped my bare arm before I could move it away. "Hot," he said, and my father asked him where he thought he was going. "Town," he said, and my father said, "You'll die of the heatstroke."

I was fourteen, beat after a day of working on our farm, and I wanted to be in our house in town—the sooner, the better—stretched out on the floor in front of the box fan, letting the air move over me. I was fourteen. I had no time for a drunk man in need of a ride.

"Let him in," my father told me, and, knowing I had no choice, I opened the door and stepped out into the weeds so he could climb in and sit between my father and me. Why didn't I just slide over next to my father and let Odie have the seat by the window? I didn't like the idea of him getting into our truck because he scared me, not because he was drunk—I realize this now—but because he was a certain sort of man common to that part of rural southern Illinois, a rough man, and I'd already started to catch on that I wasn't going to be that kind of man at all. My parents and I had come back to southern Illinois after living six years near Chicago. Our time "up north" had been long enough to distance me from the often-coarse lives of men in the small farming town where we now lived. I didn't want to be trapped between Odie and my father in that truck. I preferred whatever extra space sitting by the passenger side door would afford me.

Where'd he been? My father wanted to know, and Odie said he couldn't remember. "Somewheres, I guess." He worked a crushed package of Pall Malls out of his shirt pocket, shook out the last cigarette, and let it dangle from his lips. He reached across me to toss the empty packet out the window, and then he looked at me and said to my father, "This your boy?"

"My right-hand man," my father said. He pulled the truck back onto the blacktop and mashed down on the accelerator. We picked up speed, and soon the hot air was whipping around us, and the telephone poles were flashing by as we headed toward town. "His head's all full of girls," my father said, and I looked out the window, wishing that my father and Odie weren't talking about me, wishing I could be off by myself somewhere, which was often where I lived best in those days—inside my own head, where I was the truest person I could be, not puffed up with a swagger I didn't really feel, though I knew the company of men required it, but more the quiet, tenderhearted boy I really was, a boy more like my mother's even-tempered nature than my father's bluster. "He thinks he's a real lover boy," my father said.

That's when Odie laid his hand on my thigh. "Boy, you got any lead in your pencil?"

"Sure." I squirmed over closer to the door, but still Odie's hand clamped down on my thigh. "Yeah," I said. "I guess."

My father said in a quiet voice, "Leave the boy alone, Odie."

"Aw, I'm just having fun with Mr. Lover Boy."

"Odie," my father said, "you ought to do something about yourself. When's the last time you had a square meal?"

"I don't know." He took his hand off my leg. "Sometime a while back?" He stuck his hand in his pants pocket and pulled out a cigarette lighter. It was a stainless steel Zippo. He flipped up the lid, and I could see he'd somehow lost all the innards. There was no wick, windscreen, thumbwheel, or flint. All he had was an empty stainless steel casing. He held it up to his Pall Mall, and his thumb kept trying to find purchase, kept coming down on the rim of the casing. "Roll up that window," he told me. "I can't get my ciggie lit."

"You're off your nut," my father told him. "Take a better look at that lighter."

Odie stuck his finger into the empty casing. "I lost my goddamn lighter," he said.

By this time we were at the south end of town, coming past the first houses—the Caldwells, the Hecklers, the Griffins—and on down Christy Avenue past Sivert's Funeral Home and the Christian church and the school. We drove by the Sumner Press Office and Billy Jones's drugstore, on past the corner where Spec Atkins had his grocery on the west side and Burton Ferguson had his on the east side. My father turned left onto South Street and its short line of businesses—Piper's Sundries, Buzz Eddie's Pool Hall, Tubby's Barbershop, and Hazel and Abner's Café. My father pulled the pickup into a diagonal parking spot in front of the café.

"C'mon, Odie," he said. "Let's get you something to eat."

That was enough to shame him. "I don't need no handout. Let me out of this damn truck."

"I'd give you a five," my father said, "but you'd just spend it on a pint."

"I don't have to listen to this."

"No, you don't have to listen on account you already know what you are." My father nodded at me to open the truck door. "Go on with you, Odie. Go on and do whatever you're a mind to."

He crawled out of the truck, hitched his dirty Dickey work pants up around his bony hips, and stomped down the sidewalk, disappearing, finally, into the pool hall.

I got back into the truck, and my father and I sat there a while, neither of us saying a word.

"Don't be that kind of man," he finally said. "A no-account man." And I told him I wouldn't.

A few nights later I went on a campout with some of my friends. Who those boys were doesn't matter to the story I want to tell. They were like me. We were boys in a small town of a thousand in southeastern Illinois, boys eager to be men. We thought we knew what that meant when, really, we had no idea.

We hauled our gear to the woods beyond the railroad trestle behind my house and set up shop for the night in a clearing along the bank of a dry creek bed. We built a fire and ringed it with stones. We heated cans of Campbell's Pork & Beans in metal pans we'd borrowed from our mothers. We opened a loaf of Wonder Bread. When we were done eating, we smoked the Lucky Strikes we'd stolen from Perrott's Grocery. We turned on a transistor radio and settled back to wait for nightfall.

A gravel road ran along the edge of the woods, a little-used road that might have been something once but wasn't any longer. A car coming down that road would have to have a definite purpose. It was no route a joyrider would take. It was, instead, the sort of godforsaken road only serial killers, or someone otherwise intent on wrongdoing, would know.

If this were a work of fiction, Odie Moad would come down that road. He'd find those boys at their campsite, and maybe he'd give them all blowjobs if they'd pay him enough to score him a pint. It's all set up, after all, from the scene that opens this piece. Odie Moad laying his hand on my leg, asking me if I've got any lead in my pencil.

But that's not what happened that night at our campsite. The truth is I barely took note of Odie Moad again outside of knowing him to be here and there in our small town, a drunk man who could be nothing more than that until he was old and a resident at the nursing home where my mother worked in the laundry. It's a miracle he lived long enough to outlast his drinking, and he was so thankful he took up religion, and, when he died, he left behind a pocket Testament with a black cover and red-edged pages, and there was no one to care what he'd left except my mother, who used to talk nice to him at the nursing home and who brought that Testament home just so it would have a place to be.

The car that came down that gravel road once it was dark belonged to an older boy, a man, I suppose it would be right to say. This was in 1972. He'd done his stint in Vietnam and come back to cruise the streets of our town in his Ford LTD. He let his hair grow and his beard, and he put on a pair of aviator sunglasses, and he drove those streets, holding up his fingers in the V of a peace sign whenever he met someone. To those of us who waited that night at the campground, he was as cool as cool could be. He'd come back from the war a member of the counterculture—or at least as close as one could be in our small town. He even had a Stars and Stripes shirt, which he wore ironically. He'd had enough of war. He'd had his fill of the man. He was his own man now, cruising those streets, flashing those peace signs, answering to no one.

So, when we asked him whether he'd buy us a case of Pabst Blue Ribbon Beer and deliver it to our campground, he said, "Cool."

And that's what he did. He drove down that out-of-the-way gravel road and brought us that beer.

My father kept a bottle of whiskey in the kitchen cabinet, stuck way back in a dark corner where I wasn't supposed to find it. A fifth of Seagram's, later a pint of Old Granddad. Strictly for medicinal purposes. My father wasn't a drunk man, but he had a taste once in a while: a shot of whiskey when he was ailing; a cold Miller High Life on a hot summer day. My mother allowed it even though she was a churchgoer—a woman of modesty—even though her father had been an alcoholic. I never saw my father drunk or even the least bit tipsy, and that was a good thing because I wouldn't have wanted my mother to have the kind of life that would have brought her, the life Odie Moad's family had with him, a life of shame because he was the sort of fall-down drunk who ended up passed out on the sidewalk or singing at the top of his lungs in the middle of the night or trying to ride a kid's tricycle down the sidewalk and ending up tipped over in Miss Pixley's marigold bed. That kind of life. I wouldn't have wanted my mother to be the town drunk's wife. I wouldn't have wanted to be his son.

I have to admit, though, there was something about the liquor that caught my fancy, not only the liquor but the way, if used in the proper amounts, it could make men bigger than they actually were. It could give them more heart, more spirit, more pizzazz.

Perhaps my grandfather, before he finally got sober, felt exactly that—this lifting up—every time he drank. He lost a farm because he couldn't make it profitable enough to pay for itself. He leased a country store at Berryville—a crossroads village in the middle of farmland, a gathering of a few houses, two churches, and a school—and tried to make a go of Read's Square Deal Groceries, but that, too, eventually failed. On the night his heart finally gave out—he'd given up the bottle by then—he was again trying the grocery business, this time in a different location a few miles to the south, in Wabash County, a county of oil fields and logging interests and farms nestled up against the river of the same name that separated Indiana from Illinois. In every photo I have of him, his face is set in grim acceptance of the disappointment of his life, and yet there were the small pleasures I heard of from my mother—Zane Gray novels, St. Louis Cardinals baseball, a pet raccoon he fed from a baby bottle. Perhaps they gave him what the whiskey couldn't, a faith that life, even for him, could be worth more than everything he'd lost.

I never knew him. He was dead before I was a year old. I knew him later from my mother's stories and the things he left behind. My grandmother kept them in the drawer of the library table in her bedroom, and, though I wasn't to poke around there, I did. Before I started school, she kept me during the day. My mother taught school, and my father farmed, and while they were busy and before teachers of my own could claim me, I was my Grandma's boy. In her company I was for the most part a timid, well-behaved child, but I also got into my share of mischief—pulling up all the lettuce from her garden because I thought the leafy greens were weeds; breaking through her screen door with my fist because I was Mighty Mouse, come to save the day; poking around in the library table drawer because there were things there of my grandfather's, items that fascinated me, not only because they were his but also because I sensed, even at my young age, they had something to do with the way a man was meant to move through the world. A deck of Bicycle playing cards, old cigarette lighters, pipes and pipe cleaners, pocket knives and a small whetstone for sharpening them. I shuffled through the playing cards, tried to get the lighters to work, but they were dry of fluid, opened the knife blades, put the pipe stems in my mouth.

I have a photograph of my mother's cousin Basil and me sitting on chairs in my grandmother's kitchen. Basil is smoking a corncob pipe. I'm pretending to smoke a cigar, which is really one I've rolled from my modeling clay. There we sit, both of us in overalls, one leg folded over the other at the knee, two gents relaxing with a smoke. In another photograph I sit on my Uncle Homer's lap on Christmas Day. He's just opened a gift, a beer stein from

Germany, and I have my hands on it, as if I'm about to lift it to my mouth and take a good, long drink.

That night at the campground I drank and drank and drank. I drank the way I thought a man was supposed to drink, chugging one beer after another. By this time I'd had a beer here and there, mostly ones stolen from coolers kept in people's garages, but this was the first time I'd had enough to make me drunk—not just tipsy but fall-down drunk, black-out drunk, too close for comfort (I know this now) to not-waking-up drunk. When I think back to that night, I cringe at the picture of me in the light of that campfire, tilting back my head and pouring that beer down my scrawny gullet. I lost all sense of time and circumstance.

Someone passed around a joint. I'd never smoked grass, had told myself I never would, but there I was sucking the smoke into my lungs, holding it there, the way Mr. Cool told me, not knowing that it was all a joke. The "joint" was one of our Lucky Strikes, but I was too drunk to know the difference.

So drunk that I finally got sick all over my sleeping bag and my friends had to put me in someone else's. So drunk I rolled into the smoldering ash of the fire sometime during the night and someone had to pull me out. So drunk that come morning, when I woke and knew exactly what I'd done, my first instinct was to confess it all.

"I'm going home," I said.

The campground, in the light of day, was an atrocious testimony to the night before: the dry creek bed littered with crushed PBR cans, the cold ashes of the fire, my sleeping bag soiled and stinking of vomit. My head was still spinning a little, and I had the dry heaves. It was Sunday morning—I could hear the bells at the Christian church—and I was on my hands and knees in the dust, retching.

All I wanted to do was to get away from that place as fast as I could. I wanted time to go back to where it was before I took that first beer and started down the road to becoming this no-account, sick-as-a-dog, Sunday morning drunk that I was, and, because I knew I couldn't make that happen, the only other thing I could think to do was to come clean.

"You can't do that," one of my friends said. "You can't go home. You're still drunk."

I was clear-headed enough to know what I was doing. "I'm going home," I said again, and this time I was close to tears, stirred with shame and humiliation and something awakening inside me that I wouldn't have called love then but will now, here safe on the other side of my ignorance. Home, I kept saying to myself as I scrambled up the embankment of that railroad trestle and down the other side. Home, I said, as I went on through the field toward our house, where I intended to tell my parents exactly what I'd done.

In our house my mother and father were ready for church. My father sat at the kitchen table, reading the *Evansville Courier*. My mother stood at the counter tucking a handkerchief into her pocketbook. The kitchen still smelled of their breakfast—the eggs and bacon and the toast, slightly burned—and the morning breeze stirred the curtains at the windows by the table. When I closed the door behind me, the curtains went limp, and my mother and father turned their eyes to me.

My mother was sixty years old on that summer morning. My father was fifty-seven. Both of them were more than a bit weary with their labor—my father on our farm, my mother at the nursing home. Sunday was their one day of rest, and there I was about to disturb it. Their only child who came into their lives though they never planned on having children, and for whatever joy I brought them, I also brought them a fair share of heartache. I made their lives harder, and, for that, even now, I'm sorry.

I knew they could smell it on me, the vomit and the beer. My father said, "Jesus," and he looked at me the way he'd looked at Odie Moad, as if he wanted to put me out of his life forever.

Then my mother said my name. She said it with her sweet, measured tone of patience and endurance, and that's when I told them everything I'd come to say.

They let me talk. They let me cry and say how sorry I was, how ashamed I was. They let me tell them what a miserable sort I was, and they didn't disagree.

When I was finished, I waited for my father to light into me. He'd always been sharp with his tongue. But this time, much to my surprise, all he said was, "Where's your sleeping bag?" He said it in a tired, lackluster voice, as if he were resigned to something he'd rather not be the case.

"There." I pointed toward the railroad trestle. "It's still there."

"Go get it," he said.

I couldn't. The thought of returning to that campsite, where my friends were surely talking about what a pussy I was, what a snitch, what a lowlife, was too much for me.

"I can't," I said. "I'm sick. I'm so sick."

"Roy," my mother said, still in that measured tone, and I knew the issue was settled.

Now I understand what my father was trying to tell me, exactly what he'd tried to tell Odie Moad, that sometimes we have to face the facts of our lives. Sometimes we have to do something about ourselves. That's what it meant to be a man, this owning up.

I have no children of my own, none to break my heart or to bring me joy. I have, instead, the memory of the boy I was, that boy who was trying to figure it all out, trying to make sense of how to live a well-considered life in a land of men, so many of them put-upon by the hard work they did, trying as best as they could to keep their heads up, their hands steady, their gazes level as day after day the work on farms, in oil fields, at refineries or gravel pits, broke them down. Sometimes they turned into men like Odie Moad—drunk men, trying to absent themselves from everything that was too much for them to bear. Sometimes, like my grandfather, they saved themselves and faced the ends of their lives with whatever they carried balled up in their hearts. Sometimes, like my father, they persevered and finally slipped away, leaving their tools and their machinery behind, the wire fencing they stretched taut between posts, the earth turned over and tilled, the clay ready for another man's prints.

I'm ashamed to say I let my mother and father make the walk through that field on what should have been a glorious Sunday morning in summer. I watched them strain against the grade of that trestle embankment, too old to be doing this work, but who else was there to do it once I refused? I turned away from my duty. They couldn't. I was their son.

You Want It?

We were waiting outside Bridgeport High School one summer morning, those of us who would be going to work for the DeKalb Seed Corn Company, pulling tassels from cornstalks in their test plots to control pollination and allow new hybrids to form. I was fourteen, one of the boys from Sumner, a smaller town to the west of Bridgeport. Although there were other boys present that morning with whom I was friends, I felt out of place, a little nervous, because we were in Bridgeport, and, with more than two thousand residents, it was over twice the size of our little town. It's funny now to think of the hierarchy among the towns of that rural county in southeastern Illinois because the largest had but around six thousand people, but there's no denying it was there— an increase in population and status—Sumner, then Bridgeport, and then Lawrenceville, the county seat, laid out along the west-to-east route of Highway 250.

So there we were, Sumner boys and Bridgeport boys, about to spend three or four weeks together, every day of the week, some-

times for ten or twelve hours a day. Ample time for whatever someone didn't like about someone else to come to a boil.

Only Rick LeGrand, a Bridgeport boy, was already running
with a short fuse. Who's to say why? The surging testosterone of
a fifteen-year-old? Some bitter bone to chew? Some knock in the
teeth to make him mad at the world? All I know is that on this
morning in 1970 he was ready to whip somebody's ass.

And there was Jerry Shoulders, a Sumner boy, free from school
and about to get some cash in his pocket. He was footloose, just
dicking around on a summer morning, quick to laugh and quick
to act the fool.

He was an eighth-grader, but I'm fairly certain he'd been let
back a time or two. He was older than his peers, taller and stronger, a boy with blond hair in a bowl cut, a prominent Adam's apple, and the beginnings of a mustache and sideburns. A country
boy, rawboned and callow, stupid to the ways of the world, particularly to the fact that we Sumner boys were in enemy territory, where boys like Rick were looking for reasons to dislike us.

I was sure of that because my father's volatility had left me with
a good eye for likely trouble. At an early age I learned to be on the
lookout for anyone who might mean me harm.

Jerry, though, was happy-go-lucky, the sort of boy who might
wave his dick in the wind just to feel the breeze. He didn't care
who might be watching. I'm pretty sure he never gave Rick a
thought that morning.

"Man, I'm ready to go," Jerry said. "I'm ready to make some
moola." We were on the front lawn of the high school, some of
us sitting on a low brick wall. The sun was full up, splintering
through the branches of the tall maple trees in front of the school.
The leaves shivered whenever the air stirred, and they made a little shushing sound, the way someone would if he wanted to tell

someone else to be quiet. "Gonna pull me some tassels." Jerry's voice was loud and a little bit raspy and full of a gee-I'm-dumb-but-I-don't-know-it drawl. He was pacing back and forth, all jazzed up. "Gonna make me some cash and buy me a car. I know where I can get a '68 Chevelle at a steal. A Super Sport. Marina blue, 396 big block engine, zero to sixty in 7.4 seconds." He started making engine noises, running that dream Chevelle through its gears. "I'll put on a Hurst shifter with a steel ball." He moved his hand at his hip, imagining himself hitting second and third and then fourth. "Listen to those cherry bombs." He made rumbling and popping noises. "I'm thinking I'll put the tires on Crager rims—flash some chrome—and then I'll be sitting fine."

There were maybe twenty-five of us—some of us on that stone wall, some lying on the grass, a couple sitting on the bulldog statue of the school mascot. Just boys lazing around waiting for what was going to happen next. We were boys in sneakers and jeans and T-shirts, some of them advertising Boone's Farm or Annie Green Springs, the cheap soda pop wines that were popular then, some of them homemade tie-dyes, some of them displaying zodiac signs in bright colors, some of them just plain white tees. Other boys wore Dingo boots, and occasionally there was a pair of lace-up shoes.

Jerry wore Levis and pointy-toed cowboy boots. He had on a plaid cotton button-up shirt with the sleeves cut out and the tail flapping free. A Winston cigarette dangled from his bottom lip.

I couldn't fathom what made him want to be so loud. I'd always been shy around people I didn't know, quiet in public places. I had to get the lay of the land before I risked being heard, and one thing I knew right away that summer morning, even before Jerry started to carry on, was that Rick LeGrand was trouble.

He was broad shouldered and thick necked, and his white

T-shirt was tight across his muscular chest and around his biceps. His honey-colored hair, streaked from the sun, swept across his forehead in thick bangs that he kept tossing out of his eyes. He was a little younger than the oldest of the boys, but I could tell he ran with them, accepted because he was more physically developed than most of the boys his age, including me, who was tall but slightly built and slope shouldered, a yet to be diagnosed overactive thyroid gland rendering me rail thin. I tried to make myself small that morning so no one would notice me. I wanted to tell Jerry that he should knock it off because I could see what was going to happen if he didn't.

"Hey. Dipwad." Rick shouted from a few feet away. "You think you're a hotshot?"

Jerry kept jabbering. He was going to put on a super-charger, a Holley 750 HO carb, some 15-inch Goodyear slicks, and then run it in the sprints one day down at Haubstadt.

"You," Rick said, tromping across the school lawn.

Jerry turned around.

"I think he means you," I said.

"Me?" He pointed his finger at his chest and said to Rick, "You talking to me?"

Rick was in his face. "That's right. Who the hell do you think you are?"

"I'm Jerry." He offered his hand to Rick. "Pleased to meet you."

"Jesus." Rick knocked his hand away. "You're a fucking moron. Yakking about that Chevelle. You're not even old enough to drive, and, even if you were, you wouldn't be able to handle a car like that. Sumner's the asshole of the county, and you're what comes out of it."

Jerry tilted his head back and narrowed his eyes. "Guess it takes a turd to know a turd."

"Prick," Rick said. His right hand closed into a fist.

"Cool it," one of his friends said. "Here comes the boss."

The DeKalb man was out of his truck and was striding across the lawn in his crisp khaki work suit. He glanced down at his clipboard, ready to divide us into crews and cart us off to work.

"I'm going to put you in the hospital." Rick's voice was low now and all the more menacing for how quiet it was. "I mean it, dip-wad." He jabbed his finger into Jerry's chest. "Last day of work, I'm going to fuck you up."

My own history with fighting was scant: three set-tos, each of them consisting of one punch. Ticky-tack stuff, hardly worth playground gossip. I'd reached an age where boys were eager to prove their manhood, particularly in this place, where rough living was often the regular come-and-go; the men who worked on the farms and in the oil fields and at the refinery could be quick-tempered, particularly after a few drinks at the taverns in Bridge-port or Lawrenceville. We had more than our share of violence—not just fights of the pedestrian style but assaults and shootings and the remnants of Prohibition-era bootlegging gangs.

Our part of southern Illinois was home to the Shelton brothers, who ramrodded illegal liquor and gambling throughout Little Egypt, as this part of the state was known. Charlie Birger, Frank "Buster" Wortman, Charles "Blackie" Harris: these were all infamous figures in the struggle for power with the Sheltons. Sometimes a farmers got shot off his tractor while plowing his field. Occasionally a truck driver would be found dead in his rig, and, though carbon monoxide poisoning might be the coroner's ruling, everyone would suspect that the driver had crossed some-one he shouldn't have crossed and ended up knocked in the head.

This is all to say that I started high school in a place where disputes were often settled with fists or knives or guns. The worst thing a real man could do was to let someone else get away with something without putting up a fight.

At the time I was more bookish than many of the boys I knew—boys like Rick LeGrand—and I could be a loner, an only child who had grown accustomed to living inside a book or in my own thoughts and daydreams. I could also be sensitive, a combination of my mother's soft heart and my father's anger. The latter also gave me an inclination for causing trouble; given the right circumstances, I could do the sorts of things that gave me sway with other boys. For a while I was a shoplifter. For a while I drank too much. I went as far as a single act of arson—I was lucky no one was hurt, nor was much property damaged—before I sensed that I was about to step over a line into a place of wrongheaded living that might claim me forever.

I also happened to be athletic and extremely competitive. I loved to test my skills against other boys on the basketball court, the baseball diamond, and during sandlot football games. Our school, with only 145 students, was too small to have a football team, so on the weekends in the autumn we played pickup games, sometimes only three on three. I usually played quarterback, but for some reason one day I was centering the ball and then blocking. The rusher happened to be Jerry Shoulders.

In the midst of our wrestling and straining, him trying to get to the quarterback and me trying to prevent that from happening, something snapped inside him. After the play was over, he shoved me, and I shoved him back.

"Sonofabitch," he said. Then he made a fist and drew back his arm, ready to throw a punch.

As far as I could tell, there was no call for his anger. We'd simply been doing what we were supposed to do. Neither of us had made any sort of dirty play, no tripping, no elbow to the throat, no palm jammed up under the chin. He'd rushed, and I'd blocked. Nothing more than that.

His anger took me by surprise since he'd always been even tempered. He was so mad he made me feel like I'd done something to deserve his anger. I felt like I was in the wrong, even though I wasn't. Frustrated by his inability to get by me, he'd simply lost his temper, and now he was squared off with me, ready to fight.

I didn't want to fight him. I couldn't see what there was to fight about, and, too, he was in such a rage I was pretty sure that, had I come back at him, he would have launched into me for all he was worth. He was mad enough and strong enough to do some serious damage.

So I told him to cool down. There wasn't anything to get excited about.

"What'd I do?" I asked him, and he couldn't tell me.

"Ah, hell." He finally lowered his arm and opened his fist. He looked sheepish. "I just got pissed," he said, and I told him it was okay. No hard feelings. Let it go.

Which, to my relief, he did.

But the way Rick LeGrand muscled up to Jerry that morning in Bridgeport put me on edge, as I was those days in my home, watchful for the signs that my father was about to erupt. Although Rick had Jerry in his sights, who was to say that he wouldn't one day take a dislike to another boy just because he was from Sumner, and who was to say that this other boy wouldn't be me? Rick's presence then, and his hair-trigger temper, were enough to make me worry. Maybe I worried more than anyone else—even Jerry didn't seem all that concerned—because I knew how little it took for my father to reach for his belt, for him to leave welts on the backs of my legs.

Each day in the fields I slipped down the rows of corn, the stalks' bladed leaves cutting my bare arms and hands, and I knew that each tassel pulled, each row finished, each field, brought us closer to the last day of work and what might happen then—not just the sort of schoolboy tussle where a few punches might result in a busted lip or a black eye, but the kind of beating that would put Jerry in the hospital. I kept telling myself that surely it wouldn't happen. Surely the boss would stop it.

We had one main supervisor, a man who made it clear he had everything in line. His khaki work suit looked crisp each morning, clean and freshly pressed. One look at his Red Wing boots, and I could easily imagine him pulling the rawhide laces tight and tying them into tidy bows. He must have cleaned and polished the leather after the day's work was done because the dirt from the fields he walked was gone come morning, and the boots always shined.

His name was Tom Brandt, and most of the boys called him Mr. Brandt. He was that sort of man, the kind who deserved respect even though he didn't demand it. We understood that from the way he went about his job.

"We need to finish this field today," he told us one afternoon when we stopped for our water break. He looked up at the sky, where clouds were gathering in the west. "Storm's coming," he said, "and that's going to put us behind schedule." He tugged on the brim of his cap and squinted his eyes at us. It was a yellow cap that had the company logo on it—a flying ear of corn with green wings. Across the ear in red letters was the word *DeKalb* and below it in green letters, *When Performance Counts*. "So we need to be out of this field before we knock off." He slapped his clipboard against his leg. "Everybody got it?"

A number of us said, "Yes." Said, "Yes, sir." Said, "Yes, sir, Mr. Brandt."

He was the sort of man I didn't want to disappoint, a man who was even-keeled and fair-minded. I felt confident that, if Rick Le-Grand tried to go after Jerry Shoulders, Mr. Brandt would put a stop to it fast.

A single voice rang out after the chorus of yes-sirs died down. "You got it, Tom." Rick gave Mr. Brandt, a serious, manly nod. "All you guys hear what Tom's telling us. We got to knuckle down and get it done."

Here's the curious thing. Although Rick was far from the type of man Mr. Brandt was, I didn't want to disappoint him either. Rick was a loudmouth, a bully, an unfocused, insensitive boy, but, when he encouraged us that afternoon, I knew I didn't want him to find me lacking. I wanted to do my part to make sure we finished that field before the rains came.

Looking back on it now, part of me feels, again, that tug of the heart that I felt then, eager to stand on level ground with someone like Rick, the alpha male, but part of me feels ashamed because why should someone like him have mattered to me at all? With the wisdom of age and from the perspective of the time that's passed, I can see that he was the sort of person I would spend my adult life disdaining and disregarding, and yet, if I'm to be completely honest with myself, there's still a part of me that always wants to feel worthy of such a man's camaraderie. Like so many boys, I fought so hard to win my father's approval and, more often than not, came up short. I carried that desire with me that day in the field, and now that I'm fifty-four years old, and my father's been dead nearly twenty-seven years, I can't say that I've ever moved very far from the boy I was then. The boy gulping down his water, eager to get back to his work, wanting to feel like a man.

Then Rick nodded toward Jerry. "That means you, dipwad. No fucking off." He made a fist and shook it a little. "You know what I mean?"

Everyone knew that Rick had it in for Jerry. His threat hovered over every day of our work. Mr. Brandt knew it too. I waited for him to say something now to take Rick down a peg, but all he said was, "All right. Let's get at it."

When I think back on the weeks I spent de-tasseling corn, the experience exists in a montage of images and sensations. The cornstalks were wet with dew each morning, and the first pass down the rows left me soaked. When the sun burned off the dew, the heat and humidity settled in. I disappeared into a tunnel of cornstalks, and I pulled tassels as I went down the row. A corn plant pollinates itself from its tassel, so, in order to create hybrids, the tassels had to be pulled. Then the wind would carry pollen from nearby rows of a different variety of seed corn, and the ears that would come on the plants without tassels would be a combination of the original plant and those that provided the pollen. Only a small window of opportunity existed for this cross-pollination to take place, and that was why Mr. Brandt and the older boys—young men, really—who supervised each crew were adamant about staying on schedule.

We often worked ten- or twelve-hour days. We worked on Saturdays and Sundays. We sweated and burned in the sun, and the pollen stuck to our skin and made us itch. Our arms were covered with tiny cuts from the leaves on the stalks. We rode to the fields in a grain truck covered with a tarp. We sat on straw bales and dozed a little in the predawn dark before Mr. Brandt rousted us out and set us to work.

Midmorning and midafternoon we got a ten-minute water

break. We packed lunches with us, and I carried a thermal water jug that my mother set in the freezer each night so the water would stay as cold as possible throughout the days.

We came home in the evenings, ate our suppers, and fell into bed so we could be up at 5 a.m. We worked through rain showers, our T-shirts and jeans getting heavy from the soaking. Finally, the rain stopped, and the sun came out and heated up all that moisture, and the air was more steamy and stifling than it had been before the storm came. When there was thunder and lightning, we piled onto the grain truck and rode out the storm. Then we went back to the fields, and our boots and sneakers got caked with mud, and our steps grew heavy until we reached the end of a row and found a stick to dig at the mud and lighten our feet. We turned and went back into the corn, row after row and turn after turn, a group of boys sweeping through a field, all for the purpose of creating varieties of seed corn and all for the sum of $1.40 an hour.

This is what I chose even though I didn't have to. I chose it because, like Jerry Shoulders, I wanted the cash. I chose it because in that part of the country de-tasseling corn was a rite of passage, a step on your way to being a man. I chose it in part to have a reason to be away from my father.

He didn't discourage me from de-tasseling even though it cost him my help on the farm we still owned and worked in Lukin Township. That's how I would have spent my days those weeks if I hadn't gone to work for DeKalb. I would have helped him with the planting and the wheat harvest. I would have helped him work on machinery. I would have done things not to his liking, and he would have chided me for my shortcomings. That was our history.

I'd disappointed him that year by not going out for the high school baseball team. I was a freshman and a new boy to boot, and I was too shy around the other boys. He'd tried to force me to go out for the team, but I'd stubbornly resisted. As much as I liked playing baseball, I just couldn't bring myself to walk into that first tryout with so many boys who were strangers to me. He tried to bully me into going.

"By god, you *will* go," he said, and, though I feared his belt, which I imagined he'd soon take off and swing at me, I held my ground. Though the argument escalated, got ugly with words and curses from both of us, spiraled into the sort of family rage that shames me to recall—all in the presence of my tenderhearted mother and even my grandmother, who was living with us at the time—I refused.

I've thought about that day many times over the years, and I've come to know exactly what I knew then: It wasn't that I didn't want to play baseball—I did—but I was paralyzed by shyness and the possibility that I might fail. I'd never played organized baseball, and I felt more confident about my abilities on the basketball court. I knew I'd be able to make that team, and I decided to wait for the sure thing rather than risk being thought poorly of by the boys I hoped would accept me as their friend.

"All right, don't go," my father finally said. Then he said the words that cut me. "Just be a pantywaist all your life." *Pantywaist*—his word, archaic as it may seem now, for *sissy, pussy, pansy, wuss.*

One day at lunch Rick asked Jerry if he was queer. "Do a little cornholing with your buddies, do ya?" I knew what he meant by "buddies." I knew he meant boys from Sumner. We were sitting on the ground around the grain truck. Rick formed a circle with the thumb and forefinger of his left hand and then made the vulgar gesture of pushing his other forefinger in and out of the circle. "Like that?" he said. "Is that how you butt-buddies do it?"

We'd finished a field just before lunch and would be moving on to another, one of our last, once we were done eating. Our work was close to an end and with it the resolution—whatever it might be—to what Rick had promised Jerry that first day in front of the Bridgeport High School.

I can't remember ever talking to Jerry about his predicament. I can't recall interacting with him much at all those weeks we worked together. He wasn't on my crew, and he had his own circle of friends, a few boys closer to his age, and I had mine. I can't claim, then, any special place in his life during that time. He was a boy who liked to run his mouth, and that's what had rubbed Rick the wrong way. I kept thinking that surely he'd forget his threat. The work would take it out of him, but each day he found some way to antagonize Jerry, his ugly talk that day at lunch only the latest example. For the most part Jerry ignored him, but on this particular day, his patience wearing thin, he said to Rick, "Fuck you."

He said it in an even tone, one that told me he'd become tired of the constant badgering and was welcoming whatever might happen next just so it could be done with.

Rick dropped his hands and pushed himself up from the ground. It only took a few strides to carry him to where Jerry was sitting with his back against one of the big tires on the grain truck.

Rick grabbed him with a hand around the back of his neck and jerked him to his feet. "What'd you say?"

Jerry's shirt was unbuttoned, and his hairless chest was too white in the sun. "I said, 'Fuck you.'" His voice showed no fear, no panic. He simply stated the fact again. "Fuck you. That's what I said."

Rick put him in a headlock and ragged him around a little. One of the crew leaders, a man just a few years out of high school, said they ought to knock it off. One of Rick's friends, a boy with frizzy red sideburns, said it was just a little wrestling and nothing to get excited about.

Then Mr. Brandt came around the back of the truck and said, "All right, Rick. Let him go."

Rick slipped his arm from around Jerry's head and let it lie across his shoulders. "We were just goofing around." Rick punched Jerry lightly on his arm, a tap that might have seemed affectionate to anyone who didn't know the score. "We're friends, aren't we?"

"Sure," said Jerry. "We're buddies."

At first it made me a little sick to hear Jerry say that. Then it registered with me. He'd emphasized the word *buddies*, and, in doing so, he'd called Rick a butt-buddy. He'd called him a queer. Even Rick understood that's what had happened. He punched Jerry a little harder on the arm.

"On the truck," Mr. Brandt said. "Time's wasting. We've got work."

We climbed onto the truck, and, as we rode to the next field, Rick leveled his gaze at Jerry. "Tick-tock," he said, again and again, reminding Jerry that we only had a few days' work, and then, once there was nothing to be fired from, Rick would be able to do what he promised. "Tick-tock, motherfucker," he said. "Then you'll see who your buddy is."

When we got to our next field and climbed down from the truck, I had my thermal water jug in my hand, carrying it by the bail that served as a handle. It was one of those gallon jugs with a screw-off lid and a plastic spout to make pouring or drinking easy. It was a jug that my father and I had both drunk from when working on the farm.

For some reason, as I jumped from the truck, the handle came loose, and the water jug fell to the ground right at Rick's feet.

He looked down at it and then up at me. For a moment everything seemed to be moving in slow motion. I'd spent those weeks trying to stay out of his range, and now here I was, in his sights. "Looks like it's no good." He nodded down at the cooler. "You want it?"

Of course, there was nothing wrong with that cooler. The plastic handle had just come loose from its hinges and could more than likely be repaired. I could tell, though, that Rick so desperately wanted me to say that I didn't want that jug, and, because I was afraid to say otherwise, and though I would hate myself immediately and for years thereafter, I told him, no, I didn't want it.

He lifted his foot and drove it down onto the jug. He did it again and again with such rage that no one said a word or made a move to stop him. The jug caved in, and eventually the bottom dropped out, and the water spilled out onto the ground.

Then Mr. Brandt was there. "That your jug?" he said to me.

I nodded. "It wasn't any good," I said, and then we all went into the field.

At home that night I had to answer to my father when he asked where my water jug was. I told him the truth. I told the story exactly the way it happened. This is perhaps my only noble moment from this whole string of events. I didn't lie. I owned up to the fact that I'd let Rick stomp on that jug even though I knew it could be repaired.

"You want it?" he'd asked, and the truth was, yes, I wanted it, and the truth was, yes, somewhere inside me a small voice couldn't say what I really wanted, and, yes, there was a part of me that was afraid and a part of me that felt pleased to give Rick what he wanted for whatever pleasure it would bring him and a part of me that wanted his approval the way I always sought my father's, and there was a part of me, too, that wanted to distance myself from Jerry, or perhaps to try to save him by saying to Rick with my gift, *Here, here's our sacrifice—now please leave him alone.* All these parts of me got tangled up in an instant, and the voice that spoke didn't seem like mine at all when I told Rick, no, I didn't want it.

I didn't tell my father all of this, of course. I'm not even sure I knew it myself then, but I do now, and truth be told I feel a mix of compassion and shame for the boy I was, a shy boy trying to learn the man he would one day become. Even now, I can't quite escape that moment. I go back to it again and again. I jumped from the truck. The handle broke, and the jug fell. Rick said, "You want it?" And I told him no.

"Jesus," my father said. "You let him do that? You let him run over you that way? You're just like your mother." He shook his head and narrowed his eyes at me. "You need to learn to stand up for yourself. And that boy? That LeGrand? Someone needs to rip him a new asshole."

My father believed in force. I'm thankful that I carry enough of his fire to allow me to shoulder through the hardest spots of my life, but I have to admit there have been days when my temper has embarrassed me. It happens less frequently as the years go on, and for that I'm also thankful. I've reached a point where I've achieved a nice balance of my father's backbone and my mother's tender heart. I was trying to sort out the pull of each and where I'd eventually stand the summer Rick threatened Jerry, but I wouldn't be there the last day of work, when Rick made good on his promise.

Ashamed in my father's presence because I'd let Rick stomp that water jug, I wouldn't be able to go back to finish my work, and, of course, that would anger my father and shame me even more.

I wasn't there when Rick beat Jerry, but I'd hear the story later from my friend, who saw it all. It started on the grain truck on the last ride back to town. Rick got Jerry down in a corner and started punching. None of the other boys did anything to stop what was happening. By the time the truck rolled to a stop, Jerry's eyes were swollen shut, his lips were busted, and some of his teeth had been knocked out.

"He was fucked up," my friend said. "He couldn't even move."

They had to take him on to the hospital in Lawrenceville, where he recuperated. Some years later he and another Sumner boy, both drunk, drowned while trying to swim across a lake in the middle of the night. I suppose more often than not the reckless life comes to ruin, but I know this: He didn't deserve that beating. He was just a screwy kid in love with the idea of a '68 Chevelle Super Sport. He was just running his mouth that first morning in front of the Bridgeport High School because it was summer and he was about to have cash in his pocket. I like to think I'd have done something to stop Rick from beating him, but I'm afraid, like all the other boys, I would have kept quiet, and that's why I can't ever forget what happened. Though it was over in a week or so, Jerry's injuries healed and his life shooting ahead to the night he went under in that lake, I can't keep myself from imagining him on his back in that grain truck, Rick bearing down on him with punch after punch after punch and no one doing a thing to help him. Because I wasn't there to see it, my imagination continues to keep the moment alive, vivid and enduring over all the years that have passed.

I wish I could say I was there. I wish I could say I was a better person. All I can do, though, is recall what happened the afternoon that Rick stomped my water jug. At our afternoon water break, when each boy could drink a dipper of water from the five-gallon metal can, I was so parched I took a second dipper, even though I was supposed to wait until each boy had had one.

Rick was behind me, next in line. "Hey, dipwad," he said. "It's my turn."

I kept drinking. He made a fist and cocked his arm back. I didn't care. I drank and drank and drank until the dipper was empty.

What did I want then? Maybe I thought he'd understand that I'd let him stomp that jug and now he owed me this. Maybe it was the only way I had of telling him to fuck off. Maybe I was secretly hoping he'd let all his rage out on me and then leave Jerry alone.

When I finally gave Rick the dipper, his face was blank, as if he couldn't believe that I'd refused to give it over when he'd asked. Then he gave me a little sneer, and his voice got all tough-guy again.

"You're lucky," he said. "Lucky as shit." He pointed his finger at me. "You better remember that."

The Fat Man Skinny

Years ago my wife's aunt was in the hospital awaiting foot surgery, and the evening before the operation she phoned our home from her room. My wife answered the call and then motioned for me to pick up the extension.

"The doc was just here," her aunt said.

"What did he have to say?" my wife asked.

"He told me I was a big old beast."

"A big old beast?" My wife gave me a quizzical look. "Are you sure he told you that?"

"Yep. That's what he said. 'Mrs. Garvin, you're a big old beast. You could stand to lose a few pounds.'"

Aunt had a habit of mangling words. Once, when straight-line winds swept through Evansville, Indiana, where we all lived at the time, twisting trees from the ground, shattering windows, pulling down power lines, she called and said, "Lord, I thought Arvin Getty had come."

Armageddon, I wrote on a notepad and showed it to my wife.

Like Sheridan's famous character, Mrs. Malaprop, Aunt had a knack for choosing imposter words—deceiving, devilish words masquerading as the true ones that they had murdered and whose clothes they had stolen. They were all wrong for the context, and the results were, of course, hilarious, a fact that usually escaped Aunt. For the most part she thought she was saying exactly what she meant. Even on those rare occasions when her errors came to light, she laughed at herself. That was the way she was: bold and saucy and jolly. Despite the fact that she was now a widow, her husband having recently died after a long illness, she was a brassy, fun-loving woman who was, as the doctor chose to put it, "a bit obese."

One night, in a Sheraton Inn lounge, where she and my wife and I had gone to dance and drink Cokes spiked with the Jim Beam whiskey from the pint bottle Aunt hid in her purse, she found out that the couple at the table next to ours was celebrating their wedding anniversary.

"I'll drink to that." She lifted her glass. "This is a memoriable occasion." She looked at me. "That's a word, isn't it? Memoriable?"

"It is now," I told her. "You just made it up."

She laughed her big, booming laugh, and she swatted my shoulder hard enough to jostle me.

"Play 'Rocky Tock,'" she shouted at the band, and she started to sing her version of "Rocky Top": "Good old Rocky Tock. Rocky Tock, Tennessee."

Now I imagine what the other people in that lounge must have thought of her—loud, quick to laugh, drinking those whiskey and Cokes, doing a rendition of the song she used to perform at her country club's annual talent show, "Cigarettes and Whiskey and Wild, Wild Women." She could sure stomp and dance. Oh lord. A big old gal, but, man, she was having fun.

Now, over twenty years later, I'm having a cup of tea with a friend at a bookstore café, where the sign behind the counter says, YOUR MUSE AWAITS IN DANCING SPIRALS OF STEAM. It's a sunny, early summer afternoon, and business at the bookstore is slow. Louis Armstrong's "A Kiss to Build a Dream On"—a sleepy, bluesy tune—plays faintly over the in-store sound system, and the sunlight comes through the plate glass windows. It's a perfect afternoon for tea and Louis Armstrong and leisurely conversation.

My friend and I are talking in quiet voices. I'm telling her that my next project is an essay that has something to do with fat. A former student who's putting together an anthology asked me if I could write something on the subject, and I told him I'd try.

I should say here that my weight is average for a man my height. I'm six feet one inch tall, and I weigh 175 pounds. So my friend, a slim woman, gives me a slightly skeptical smile, as if she doesn't think there's a chance in the world that I'll have anything to say about being fat.

Still she wants to be helpful, good friend that she is, so she says, "Have you ever been fat?"

I tell her no.

"Have you ever been afraid that you might get fat?"

"Nope," I say.

These are lies I never planned on telling and that surprise me when I do. I didn't think about them. I didn't say to myself, You can't tell her the truth. She asked the questions, and, before I knew it, denials were coming out of my mouth. Right away, I wonder, What's the story here? Now here I am, writing this essay, trying to get the skinny on myself so I can figure out why I lied and what it means about the right I have, or don't have, to say anything at all about weight.

The truth is I've been fat—admittedly, not a "big old beast" like Aunt but still fat enough to make me cringe when I look at certain photos from my past. I was "chubby" in the sixth and seventh grades, "stout" toward the end of high school, "hefty" (over two hundred pounds) my second year as a married man.

My junior high basketball squad was split into two teams, the division based upon a formula that involved a boy's height and weight. I was on the heavyweight team. In the team's photo, in which we're in an arced line, I'm the one on the end, seen somewhat in profile, my belly stretching the nylon jersey fabric of my blue warm-up jacket. I remember the first time I saw that photo in our school's yearbook. I felt as if I were looking at someone else, someone who seemed familiar to me but whom I couldn't quite place. Where had that belly come from, and why hadn't I ever noted it as something a twelve-year-old boy should have preferred to be without?

It came from my mother's cooking and my healthy appetite. I hadn't given a second thought to the extra pounds I was putting on because I grew up in southern Illinois farm country at a time when such weight was the norm. I knew men with nicknames like Tick and Tubby and Bear Grease and Moose. A hearty man carried a hearty weight.

Even when we left the farm for Oak Forest, we carried with us our customs with food. We came from people who cooked with lard; deep-fried donuts, catfish, breaded mushrooms; pan-fried almost anything you can think of and some things you might not imagine: bologna, potatoes, corn cakes, ham, hot dogs, chopped steak, corn mush, cucumbers, chicken, spam. We ate lunch meat sandwiches on white bread: pickle loaf, olive loaf, braunschweiger—often with thick slices of cheese. We covered our meat and potatoes with milk gravy made from bacon drippings. We poured half-and-half over bowls of blackberry cobbler; scooped mounds of Prairie Farms vanilla ice cream, slightly yellow with butter fat, onto slabs of apple pie, red velvet cake, German chocolate cake. We whipped cream and ate it with pumpkin pie or gingerbread. We drank buttermilk, soda pop, ice tea with sugar sludging the bottom of the glass. For a snack we slathered cake icing on graham crackers, made sandwiches from butter and strawberry preserves, spread honey over cinnamon toast.

If you didn't eat—if you were "off your feed," as my father would say of a cow or a horse—it was a sign that you weren't working hard enough; it was a disgrace. "He's a good eater," people would say of someone when they wanted to tell you exactly what kind of man he was, if they wanted to give you a measure of his character. *A good eater.* Enough said.

We can be starving no matter our size. We can hunger for love, attention, money, dignity, hope. We can be desperate to feel full. Aunt, when she was a widow, was starving for companionship. Those strangers who saw her out and about nights at the hotel lounges near the airport or downtown at the Captain's Den or out Columbia Avenue at Peg's Piano Bar thought they knew exactly who she was: big, old, fun-loving gal. Pint bottle in her purse. Lord-a-mercy, she was a party girl. Betcha she could sure keep you warm at night.

But they didn't know that sometimes in the evening she'd call on the telephone and say, "It's me," and her voice would be dull and weary, not the arm-slapping, good old Rocky Tock yee-haw she shouted in those lounges and bars. The people who saw her stomping and dancing, and who sometimes stomped and danced along with her, had no idea that inside she was puny. "What're you doing?" she'd say on the phone, and, when the conversation started to lag, all matters ordinary and everyday hashed out, she wouldn't say good-bye. She'd hold on, through long stretches of silence, as if she were a speck of nothing on the other end of that line, the sound of her breathing the only evidence that she was still there, waiting for me or my wife to say something else—anything—so we could go on talking, filling up the minutes of her lonely nights.

Then she found a man, or maybe he found her, but, anyway, there they were, the two of them, and suddenly she was in business. He was fat every which way you can think of fat. Fat of belly and jowls, fat with ego, fat with money, fat with time. Living off the fat of a family inheritance, he drove fat cars, wore fat rings, ate fat steaks, talked fat dreams. He was, as my father would have said, "as full of shit as a Christmas turkey."

He barreled into Aunt's life, and right away she was head over heels. Over the next twenty years, once they were married— though some say they never legally tied the knot so she could go on drawing her first husband's pension—she'd swallow Uncle Fat Cat's schemes, believe the wildest stories, agree to the most far-fetched ideas, all for the sake of his company and the way he made her feel like every day was a Macy's Thanksgiving Day Parade and they were helium balloon figures floating overhead, so full—so absolutely and luxuriously full—they could barely keep themselves from drifting off to heaven. He talked her into selling her home and traveling around the country with him in an obscenely large recreational vehicle, the kind he drove from a leather-padded captain's chair. When he got tired of playing with that, he had a house built out in the country and then complained about the smell of the neighbor's hog farm. I've lost count of how many homes they've owned since selling that one, how many Lincoln Town Cars he's bought, how much jewelry he's given Aunt. They keep moving and buying. It appears that whatever he wants Uncle Fat Cat can afford. I suppose Aunt is happy with their life, although, of course, I've never asked her. In fact, my wife and I never see her and Uncle Fat Cat these days. A few years back at Christmas, when he was all puffed up, telling the story of how he was trying to sell their house without involving a realtor, he said that, if someone called and asked how much he wanted, he told them not to waste his time.

"If they have to ask," he said, "they can't afford it."

My wife, who with good cause had always disliked his arrogance and pomposity, had finally had enough. "You," she told him, "are full of bullshit."

That was it, he said. "Get your things," he told Aunt. "We're leaving, and we're never coming back."

Aunt did as he said, and that was the last time my wife and I saw them.

The first time I met him—he and Aunt and my wife and I were having dinner at a steakhouse—he told me that in 1975 he'd been abducted by aliens. He'd been driving across the Ohio River bridge from Evansville to Henderson, Kentucky, and right in the middle of the bridge a spaceship landed in front of him, and aliens took him aboard.

"See this?" He tugged his trouser leg up over his calf and pointed to a spot. "See those radiation burns? They performed some sort of experiment on me. Then they let me go."

I couldn't see a thing, but I nodded, as did my wife, both of us so anxious for Aunt to escape her loneliness that we were willing to hand her over to this man. People can be fat with fantasy, delusion, insanity, or, as in the case of Uncle Fat Cat, an overabundant desire for importance.

Aunt was nonplussed. She was checking her lipstick in her compact mirror. "Isn't that something?" she said. "Aliens." Then she snapped the compact shut.

One evening, when I was in high school, I was sitting at our kitchen table eating a bowl of ice cream. I wasn't wearing a shirt, which I thought was my right, on a warm evening in my own house where I could sit, content, enjoying that vanilla ice cream.

An acquaintance of my father's was in the living room discussing some sort of farm business. I didn't know this man very well. Now I can't even remember his name. I do recall, however, with painful clarity, the moment he came into the kitchen to say hello. He stopped in the doorway, his hands on his hips, and he studied me a good long time. Then he said, "My God. Would you look at that boy's gut?"

We can think we know who we are. Through all manner of hope and self-deceit we can convince ourselves that we're the people we most want to be. Then someone like this man comes along and with one look, one statement, makes it plain exactly how the world sees us.

A curse on people like that, the ones who make us doubt ourselves, the plainspoken ones who burrow into our psyches and sometimes stay there, repeating evil words the rest of our lives. If I could, I'd starve that man away, but I can't any more than my wife can forget the man who, at a campground, when she was thirteen, said to her, "You're a little fatty, aren't you?" She remembers these exact words, calls them up from time to time, and, when she says them, I can feel the immutable pain in her voice. "He didn't even know me," she says. Now, whenever she looks in the mirror—when she mourns this added pound or that—how can she help but hear that man's voice, a stranger who came into her life for just that moment and flung demonic words that still haunt her?

There's a photo of me from the second year of our marriage. I'm sitting on the floor in our attic apartment, opening a Christmas present—a Lava Lite whose red gobs of wax, when heated, will float in liquid. By this time I'm fat; there's no other word for it. My belly hangs over my belt. Fat rolls line my waistline. My ass has spread beyond the bounds of acceptable assdom. It's no trick of the camera; I am, like the Lava Lite, oozing goo. This fact came as a shock to me, the first time I saw that snapshot; until then I'd somehow convinced myself that I was just a little thick around the waistline, not fat. The snapshot, though, made me look at myself the way a stranger would.

How much do our bodies define us? Of course, our self-image depends somewhat on the person we see when we look in the mirror and the identity other people pin on us. But isn't it wonderful to think that there's always another person inside, a spirit formed during those early years of childhood, that dances on, like Aunt stomping to good old "Rocky *Tock*," unwilling to take that mirror's image or that other person's comment as gospel?

Shortly after that Christmas photo was taken, I was in a game of playground basketball, and a friend, disgusted with my sluggish moves, my slow play, said, "Man, what's happened to you?"

That day on the basketball court with my friend I didn't want to admit that I had become this lava stranger—thick and slow of foot. So, even though inside I knew it was too late—my friend's question was rhetorical; the answer was already plain—I tried to pretend that what he saw before him was simply what happened as the years went on.

"Brother." I patted my belly. "Nothing but that good, married life."

I was ashamed to admit that I was fat. I didn't know then that eventually I'd get my weight under control.

Now, when I think back to the times in my life when I was fat, I do so with a certain amount of unease. I recall a particular moment on the school playground when I was that chubby seventh-grader. I was playing touch football, and another boy noticed my short-stepped, swaying gait. My weight made me toddle—rockety-rock, like a duck.

"Hey, look at him waddle," the boy said.

"Waddles," said another. "Hey, Waddles."

In that instant the nickname stuck. The moment stunned me. How quickly it had happened. I'd never felt this waddling motion in my walk. I'd never known this thing about myself. It didn't do any good that I protested and tried to bully the ugly word out of the boys' mouths, told them to shut the hell up, shoved at them. They just danced out of my way, nimble and light bodied, and there was nothing more I could do. I was Waddles.

"Quack-quack," a boy said, and the others chimed in. "Quack-quack."

Of course, this should be such a trivial moment now, this adolescent teasing, and in a way it is, an amusing anecdote, a memory that has nothing to do with the man I am today. At least that's the lie I try to tell myself, not wanting to admit that after thirty-six years those boys' taunts still have the power to sting. "Waddles," they called me, and Waddles I was. They made me ashamed of myself, one of the worst sins we can visit upon another human being. They stole part of my spirit away, part of the essence I carried inside, and made everything about me, in my eyes, suspect.

So here's the straight stuff, the truth I should have told my friend that day in the bookstore café, the real skinny I would have spun had my muse actually awaited in dancing spirals of steam. Sometimes now, as the years go on and my waistline thickens a tad, I'll look in the mirror and think, Well, here he comes. I fear that the fat man I've spent my life escaping and then trying to avoid waits only for the slightest opportunity to reemerge. I worry that if this happens, if this familiar shape one day again fills my mirror, this time he'll be here to stay, and how will I ever be able to make friends with him—this chub, this fat cat, this Waddles, this big old beast of myself that the world has taught me to hate?

If I'd said these words to my friend, they would have taken on substance and weight; they would have put the image of me as a fat man in her mind. Instinctively, bent on self-preservation, I lied to keep that from happening. I didn't even know that I carried this shame inside me, not until she asked her questions and I heard myself saying, No, I'd never been fat; no, I wasn't afraid that one day I might be. That was a story I didn't want to tell, a confession I wasn't ready to make.

I've had to come home, close the door to my writing room, and privately, secretly, say this all to myself, swallow it all again—all the embarrassment and ridicule, all the bulky, burdensome memories of being fat.

Now I think of Aunt and her long silences during those telephone conversations. I shake my head over all the things we can't say, all the secrets we carry around, all of us swollen with worry over what the world might think of us. I'm ashamed that I lied to my friend. I've had to write this to claim the whole weighty truth of myself, and what troubles me now is how quickly and easily I lied, as if my former fat self, always in control, was whispering in my ear, *You can't tell. Don't tell. You can't ever tell.*

Who Causes This Sickness?

One day when I was fifteen my aunt announced, "This boy's got too much thyroid." She had noted the swelling in my throat, my weight loss, my bulging eyeballs.

Off to the doctor I went. I sat on his examination table, my legs swinging, my heels banging the table's metal end; I was always jazzed in those days—restless, irritable, unable to sleep through the night. The doctor stepped up close to me. His first name was Gilbert, which I thought was the sort of name a very decent man would have. He put his hands on my knees, and I stopped swinging my legs.

"Are you nervous?" he asked. He was trim, with a thick head of brown hair, parted neatly on the side, the sort of man who would have looked spiffy in a Brooks Brothers suit and penny loafers. I'd heard he had once been an army doctor, and I could believe it. He looked spit shine and by the rules in his navy blue slacks, the creases down the legs razor-sharp; his polished black oxfords; his white medical jacket, the knot of his necktie poking out over the top.

"Nervous?" I asked.

He put his hand to my throat, and his fingers pressed my wind-pipe. "You seem a little on edge." He stared at me over the tops of his half-glasses, looking first at one eye, then the other.

It was 1970, and, though our small southern Illinois town was filled with coarse men, it also had its share of men like the doctor, men who were stalwart and beyond reproach, standard-bearers of right living: the basketball coaches, the principal, the bank tell-ers, the shoe salesmen, the ministers. I envied the confident and easy way they moved through the world. I despised the way they looked at me and—so I believed—found me derelict and wanting.

And I was. I was a shoplifter, a burglar, an arsonist. I stole from stores. I broke into schools and garages. I set fires. I had never meant to become this kind of person, but, after years of endur-ing the storm of my father's rage, I had begun to express my own anger. I had careened into a life I couldn't have imagined the year before, when I had been a straight-A student and captain of the freshman basketball team. Part of me reveled in my new iden-tity, and part of me wanted to conceal it from the world, particu-larly from men like this doctor, whom I secretly wanted to please.

He kept staring at me. How can anyone, no matter how kind and well-meaning, study you over the tops of half-glasses and not appear critical?

Finally he let go of my throat and took a step back. He held out his hands, palms up, and told me to put mine on top of his. "Relax your fingers," he said. "Don't be so stiff." He slid his hands back until his fingertips were below my own, touching them ever so slightly. I've never forgotten the brush of his skin against mine. It was a tickle, like the wings of a butterfly if it were to settle on your cupped palm, wings opening and closing, skimming your curled fingers.

The moment was so delicate and intimate that I suddenly felt shy. I wanted to pull my hands away and hide them, for now my fingers were trembling and skittering about. I tried my best to hold them still, but I couldn't. I bowed my head, ashamed. My body had betrayed me, revealing that I was damaged goods. Though I was a hoodlum, I still had enough conscience to feel guilty. I believed that my body's breakdown was a clear sign of my diseased soul.

Before Hippocrates and his *Corpus*—a collection of some sixty medical treatises that marked the birth of modern medicine—the ancient Greeks investigated illness by asking the question "Who causes this sickness?" The answer was often a capricious or malevolent deity. Then Hippocratics dissolved this notion, professing instead the theory that the human body was composed of four humors: blood, phlegm, black bile, and yellow bile. If these fluids lost their natural balance, illness would result. From that point forward physicians sought to explain sickness naturally rather than supernaturally.

Still, the suspicion lingered among the religious that the body's ills were evidence of the soul's imperfections. Although illogical, this belief in God's punishment illustrates how difficult it is for the healthy to empathize with the unwell and how wide the gap can be between the two.

At the time my thyroid gland was overactive, I knew a young man named David, who went to my family's church. David was a few years out of high school and newly married to a girl with a bright, round face and a pleasant smile. He was the second of four brothers. The other three had inherited their mother's red hair, her weak knob of a chin, her freckled skin, her cackling laugh.

They were, my father often said as we drove home from church, a bubble past center, a few bricks shy of a load. "That David," he said, "he's the only one of those boys who's got a lick of sense."

David had his father's blond hair, which he kept neatly trimmed and combed. His skin was smooth and golden in summer, and his arms were muscled from farmwork. Even now, when I see fair-haired Mormon missionaries riding their bicycles down the street, their white shirts gleaming in the sun, I think of David. He often assisted with the church services—reading Scripture, leading prayers, serving Communion—and, when he walked to the pulpit, his step was confident, his spine straight, his posture erect. When he came down the aisle, holding the serving tray with its thimble-sized cups of grape juice (Christ's blood) or the silver platter with its cracker square (Christ's body), he did so with an easy grace. He was comely and devout, at peace in the small church, where each Sunday voices rose up in song and preachers invited the lost to "come home." The building itself was modest and plain, a clapboard box with a gambrel roof, but it was meant to be a place of miraculous redemption, a holy house where the penitent could be saved.

One Sunday, during the hymn that preceded the preacher's sermon, David started to tremble. He was sitting a few rows up from my mother and father and me, and we were singing "In the Garden," when suddenly the hymnal began shaking in his strong hands. He leaned forward at the waist, and his hymnal rapped the back of the pew in front of them. His wife put her hands on his arms to hold them still.

We kept singing:

And he walks with me
And he talks with me
And he tells me I am his own.

But really we were watching, some of us stealing glances and others making no attempt to hide our curiosity. David was rocking back and forth. He shook off his wife's hands, folded his arms across his chest, and tried to pin them down himself, but he couldn't. Then his head fell back, his eyes closed, and he crashed to the floor, his body convulsing so violently that his legs and arms banged against the pews.

His father and older brother came quickly to try to hold him still. When he was finally calm, they carried him from the church. His eyes were closed, his body limp. As they passed our pew, his dangling hand brushed my arm.

Our singing had stopped. The preacher came to the pulpit and scolded those who had gawked at this unexpected and horrific episode. He was a tall man, well over six feet, and he had a rich baritone voice that at that moment was the voice of authority. "The family is seeing to what's happened," he said. "Our job is to be with God." Then he said a prayer for David and his family and began his sermon.

For a good while thereafter I couldn't get the image of David's flailing body out of my mind. Ordinarily the embodiment of grace and ease, he had twitched and writhed. He had become chaos and spectacle. If it could happen to him, it could happen to anyone. None of us was safe. What affected me most was the fact that his disintegration had occurred in public; we would never be able to look at him again without remembering the way he had come apart.

It happened again the next Sunday and the Sunday after that and several Sundays running.

The rumor was that the doctors could find no physiological explanation for the seizures, and the theory began to spread that David was possessed, that demons were at war for his soul.

By this time I was taking an antithyroid drug that was blocking my thyroid's hormone production and returning balance to my system. Consequently, I believed in rational explanations for the body's ailments. Still, a part of me couldn't help thinking that what people said about David might be true: that he had become weak in spirit and had invited demons to fill him. After all, his seizures occurred only in church—a sign, some said, that he was tortured by guilt. No matter the physiological or psychological reasons, he was on display and, as a result, had become the object of our pity and curiosity and tenderness and disgust. On those Sundays when his seizures overcame his self-control, there was nowhere for him to hide. Watching him, I, too, felt exposed. I feared that my shy glances were proof that I shared his condition; that I, like David, was wicked.

When I was forty, I began to suffer corneal erosions. My left eye went dry, as if I were a man twice my age, and at night, as I slept, my eyeball scraped against the inside of my lid and scratched away minute bits of tissue from the cornea, leaving furrows visible only in the glaring light of an ophthalmologist's slit lamp. Night after night I awoke screaming in pain.

Imagine a grain of sand in your eye and then magnify that sensation a thousand times. Imagine someone rubbing sandpaper or an emery board over your eyeball. Imagine rust, salt, mud when it's dried and cracked and flaked. Imagine all of this in your eye and no way to wash it out.

I've kept myself from writing about my eye because I haven't been able to muster the courage to revisit those days. I haven't wanted to see myself again, crouching on the floor, my eyelids fluttering: wanting to close, wanting to open, each position agony. I've had no desire to hear again the growls in my throat, the keening whine, the sounds a wounded animal would make. I've tried to forget the urge to claw at my face or to beat my head against the floor—anything to stop the pain. My body has spent years attempting to unlearn this misery, wary of any reminder, anxious to flee. To call it up now fills me with fear and dread, but I can't look away. I'm a rubbernecker at my own misfortune, and I don't know what to feel. I want the horrible memory gone, and at the same time I want to describe it to you, every bit of it. I want to describe it to myself. I went to sleep every night for a year unsure of my rest, knowing that sometime before dawn I would likely wake with a start, my eye scraped and bloodshot, the world a blur to me, as if it wavered behind a curtain of fire.

"Hold your eyes open and look into the light," the ophthalmologist told me when I finally sat in his examination room.

My chin rested in the cup of the slit lamp's support. The room was dark, but the lamp's intense light blazed through its narrow opening and penetrated my left eye. It was a blinding white light: the glare of sun on chrome, the burst of a camera's flash, the brilliance of snow cover on a sunny day. It was impossible to stare at for long. When the ophthalmologist finally swung the slit lamp away from my face, I was relieved.

"Mr. Martin," he said, "you're experiencing erosions of your cornea." He said this cheerfully, as if celebrating how quickly he had been able to diagnose the problem.

The diagnosis interested me only if he could answer two further questions: First, why was my cornea eroding? And, second, what would happen if the condition persisted?

"Your eyes are very dry." The ophthalmologist wore a long white lab coat. When he sat on his swivel stool, the hem of the coat nearly touched the floor. "You should start using liquid tears and an ointment at bedtime."

"Will that stop the erosions?"

The wheels on the stool squeaked as the ophthalmologist rolled over to his desk. "Well, we'll certainly hope so."

"And if it doesn't?"

He looked up from my chart. "The good news is the cornea is the fastest healing part of the body."

"But I don't want my cornea to be injured at all. *Corneal* and *erosion* are two words I don't ever want to hear together."

There were treatments, he explained, but they were tricky, given the fact that, once the cornea has eroded, the eyelid is more likely to catch on the scar tissue, thereby reinjuring the surface. The key is to give the cornea time to heal completely, leaving the surface smooth. The first step would be to fit me with a clear contact lens to be worn for six months. After the lens was removed, the ophthalmologist could insert plugs into the openings beneath the bottom eyelid, where excess tears drained, thereby irrigating the eye more fully. If neither of these options worked, he said, he could do a corneal implant—take away my old cornea and start anew.

"I'll try the liquid tears," I said.

"Good luck," he told me, again with that smile I desperately wanted to trust.

All of this was happening in Harrisonburg, Virginia, in the middle of the beautiful Shenandoah Valley, where my wife, Deb, and I had moved so I could teach a year at James Madison University. The mountains and the forests, splendid with color come fall, had drawn us from the flat plains of Nebraska, where the prior autumn my eyes had been tremendously dry. I had rubbed at them while trying to read, had splashed them with water. But I'd always slept through the night. Then, when winter came, the problem disappeared and didn't return until we moved to Harrisonburg. The year we spent there was pure anguish.

Although I had long ago outgrown my adolescent inclination toward criminal behavior and was now one of the good citizens I'd secretly wanted to please when I was a teenager, I still felt morally suspect when this chronic condition appeared like a scourge levied against sin. Yes, it was illogical, but I couldn't help but wonder about my own culpability. With the move and the pressures of fitting into new surroundings and performing well at a new job, my nerves were often on edge. Perhaps I was too worried, too fretful, too pessimistic, and had caused a breakdown in my own immune system.

If not for Deb, I would have been completely miserable. She was the only person I could look to for empathy. But even she couldn't understand the pain I felt when my cornea eroded. It was unlike any pain I had ever experienced—including the time when I was a child and I fell running up the porch steps and cracked my tooth on the cement and the time my cousin accidentally hit me in the eye with the swing of his baseball bat. To make matters worse, I was frantic with frustration because there was nothing I could do to protect myself. It hurt to keep my eyes open; it hurt to close them. I was totally helpless.

Because Deb couldn't grasp the pain, she couldn't understand the crazed way I behaved when I was experiencing it. "It was hell," she tells me now when I ask her what she remembers of those days. "Sometimes you acted like you were crazy." (I was. Crazy with pain.)

Imagine that you have lain down beside your husband or wife and fallen into the timeless drift of sleep only to be shocked awake by your partner's anguished screams. How do you accept the sight of him or her turned into a lunatic? To Deb it must have seemed that she had awakened to a Greek tragedy: Oedipus gouging out his eyes; Prometheus, bound and unable to protect himself from the vulture's pecking. How could she make sense of the fact that I, who had first come to her so shyly and tenderly, was now a savage, raging against a pain that she couldn't take upon herself and make ours?

One night, during an attack, she spoke harshly to me. I was on my hands and knees on the bedroom floor, weeping, calling out to God, growling, jerking my head about. "Oh, stop it," she said. "Don't be so hysterical."

She said it as if she were an annoyed and impatient stranger, and I felt wounded and betrayed. I understood for the first time that my pain was mine and mine alone. No one would ever feel it with me, not even the person I loved the most.

"I wasn't mad at you," she tells me now. "I was just angry because I couldn't do anything to make you better."

When I wasn't in pain, I couldn't stop thinking about the time my cousin hit me in the eye with that baseball bat. I remembered the way my eye swelled—it would have been my left eye, given the fact that my cousin batted right-handed. The ophthalmologist had told my mother to keep warm compresses on the eye to reduce the swelling. When she laid the warm washcloth on my eye, I'd felt a pain very similar to the pain I experienced when I crawled on the floor, keening, and Deb could do nothing to save me.

The liquid tears didn't work; the corneal erosions continued. Winter came, and again the problem vanished. How sweet were those few months when I was able to enjoy the sort of mindless rest I had taken for granted for so many years. How grand it was to hold Deb close throughout the night, the heat of her body soaking into mine. Once again, I could relax and wake each morning refreshed.

Then spring erupted. The crocuses and daffodils and hyacinths bloomed. Leaves unfurled, and the trees were bright green with new growth. The air was redolent with the scents of the moist earth, wild onions in the pastures, pines and cedars on the mountain slopes. Deb and I slept with our windows open.

One morning, around four o'clock, I felt the familiar grit in my eye, and soon I was writhing on the floor.

"It's allergies," I told Deb when the pain had finally eased. "It has to be allergies."

"It can't be allergies," the ophthalmologist said when he examined me from his swivel stool. "If it were allergies, you'd be having the problem in both eyes."

Why then, I asked him, was my condition always worse in autumn and spring? And why in winter, when the trees and flowers and grasses were dormant, did the erosions stop?

"Mr. Martin, your condition could have a number of physiological causes. Perhaps your general practitioner could help you."

"My general practitioner sent me to you."

The ophthalmologist took a breath and let it out. "Yes. Well."

It was clear that he had little interest in diagnosing the cause of my condition; he was more comfortable with treating it. "We could always try the plugs," he said.

It was a tempting offer, I'll admit. Why not try any method of treatment on the chance that it might work? What was it that kept me from saying, "Yes, the plugs. Let's give them a go"?

I could tell you that ever since my cousin had hit me with that baseball bat, I had been squeamish about my eyes. I had never even been tempted to wear contact lenses because I couldn't bear the thought of touching anything to my eyeballs. I even had trouble holding my lids open long enough to put in the liquid tears. The ophthalmologist's exams with his slit lamp were torture. The thought of any surgical procedure involving my eyes, such as the one to insert the plugs, appalled me.

All of this is true, but it isn't the whole story. It's the story I told myself then, not knowing that there was another narrative running beneath it: the story of my father and me and our history of suffering.

Because my father lost his hands in that farming accident, who could blame him for believing, the rest of his life, that the world could turn on you at a moment's notice?

As I grew into young adulthood, I came to believe that one day I would suffer a tragedy like his. I suppose I prophesied this as a way of empathizing with him. I imagined myself in his place, experiencing, in some way, his suffering. In my father's case the doctor's course of action was immediately clear: amputation. There was nothing my father could do about it. With my own condition I had more control. I could accept or reject my doctor's suggestion.

So, when the ophthalmologist suggested the plugs, I said no. My logic was simple: I feared the surgery and thought there surely must be a simpler solution to my problem. I guess I hadn't hit rock bottom yet. I wasn't desperate enough. I was also dangerously susceptible to the seduction of chronic illness, the place where we become so intimate with our pain that we begin to believe that we were meant to have it. Little by little it wears away our former healthy life and becomes the only life we have. How can we help but embrace it while at the same time longing to be free from its hold? I said no to the ophthalmologist because I couldn't bear the thought of surgery. I didn't know then that there was more to my refusal than what I was telling myself.

Until the nineteenth century, when Kraft-Ebbing and Freud defined masochism as a pathological aberration, civilization celebrated the connection between physical suffering and spiritual

rapture. Suffering was essential to transcending the ego and unit-
ing with the will of a higher power. Pain allowed one to become
more human. "Humiliation is the way to humility," Saint Francis
of Assisi said, "and without humility, nothing is pleasing to God."

As a boy, I learned about physical pain and humiliation from
my father, who was always quick to discipline me with his belt. I
came to believe that I deserved his whippings because I provoked
his anger with my petulance.

One day my father refused to permit me to accompany my second-grade classmates on a field trip to the amusement park at Santa
Claus, Indiana. It cost too much money, he said—money he didn't
have to spare—and he didn't want to hear another word about it.

"Please, Daddy," I said.

He pointed his hook at me. "Not another word."

"But I want to go," I said.

"Mister, I'm warning you. You're breeding a scab on your ass."

We were in the machine shed, where my father was getting
ready to climb up on his tractor. I threw a tantrum, crying and
whining. When that got me nowhere, I picked up a corncob and
threw it, striking him on the side of his face.

I ran to the house, but there was nowhere to hide, and soon my
father was there, his belt already undone and grasped between the
pincers of his hook. He lashed me about my legs as I tried to jump
away. I was screaming, desperate to make him stop.

"I'll be good," I said. "I'll be good. Please, Daddy. I'll be good."

When he was finally done, I lay on my bed sobbing, my legs
stinging from the belt's bite.

This scene repeated itself countless times when I was a boy, and
each time, when the world finally returned to normal—when my
father and I were both calm and ashamed—I would go to him and
say, "I love you, Daddy." Sometimes there were tears in his eyes,

and his voice trembled. "All right," he said. "All right." I sensed that he was saying, the only way he could, that he was sorry.

I believe we reached these moments of contrition because we had touched what Jung calls "the shadow"—the archetype for the part of the self that is weak, sinful, degraded. My father and I were both sorry for our behavior, and, until his anger erupted again, we would be shy around each other, and sweet, as if we could love more fully because first we loved so poorly and caused so much pain.

As difficult as it is for me to admit, I still can't help but wonder whether I unconsciously agreed to the corneal erosions. They were my burden, one that perhaps, in the illogical realm of the psyche, I was content to carry.

How else can I explain the fact that, not long after the oph-thalmologist suggested the plugs, I rejected my general practitio-ner's proposal to test my thyroid function? I was still convinced that my problem was caused by allergies. Perhaps, I told my GP, a prescription antihistamine might be worth a try.

My doctor wore tailored suits, like a bank executive, and she wrote with a thick, expensive-looking pen. "I'd never prescribe an antihistamine for you," she said. "It would dry you out."

"So you think it might be my thyroid?"

"Might be," she said. "Or it could be something else. Maybe Sjögren's syndrome."

"Sjögren's? How do you spell that?"

"I'm not sure. I'll have to look it up."

She left the examining room and returned a short time later with a thick medical reference book. "Found it," she said. She spelled the name and started to read: "In Sjögren's syndrome, changes occur in the immune system. White blood cells invade glands in the body that produce moisture, such as the tear and salivary glands, destroying these glands and impairing their function."

Watching her with that book, I thought of shade tree mechanics poring over automotive manuals or kids trying to figure out directions for a model airplane kit. When she stopped reading and looked at me, I imagined that she was seeing dotted lines on my body, the way a butcher marks a side of beef.

"It's very difficult to diagnose," she said.

"And the cure?"

"There isn't any. But don't worry. We can manage it. You'll be fine. It's more of a nuisance than anything else. We can treat the symptoms."

"Liquid tears?"

She nodded. "And there are plugs to block tear drainage. Your ophthalmologist can tell you about that. In the meantime we should check that thyroid. Yes?"

All it would have taken was a simple blood test, a prick of a needle, and then a lab report. The science of blood analysis would have told my doctor whether my thyroid gland was functioning properly.

It would be easy, and cowardly, to say that I refused because my GP, her medical reference book open on her lap, seemed inept or because my medical insurance wouldn't pay for the blood test or because I had accepted a job in Texas and thought, Why pursue this now? Why not wait to see whether a change of climate might cure me?

Despite my misery, I used all these reasons to turn down another treatment option. Crazy? Of course. Wrongheaded? Absolutely. How can I explain my decision? As much as it pains me to admit it, I said no to the thyroid test because some secret part of me fancied the idea of Sjögren's syndrome. It was exotic and incurable, a nuisance to wear the rest of my life, the way my father had slipped into the harness of his hooks each morning, rolling his shoulders to settle the canvas straps across his back. I didn't think this at the time, but it makes sense to me now. Why else, at the offer of a potential cure, would I choose to remain a victim?

Suffering was my family's habit. No matter the ways we found to enjoy life—and there were many—my father's hooks were a constant reminder of loss and ache. I remember the creases they left on books and magazines and newspapers, the scrapes they gouged into the wooden handles of hoes and shovels and rakes, the marks they made on chair arms and sofa cushions and door-knobs. Even after his death there were these reminders of his burden, which in a way became my mother's burden, and mine, too. It never leaves me, the fact that my father had no hands, that he wore those hooks. Sometimes, when I find myself slipping into depression or self-pity, I fear it's because that's the only way I have to love him now that he's dead—to let myself feel his misery, to imagine how he must have felt after his accident. When I was a teenager and there was so much anger between us, it was difficult for me to understand the way the world must have looked to him: suspect and dangerous. Any act of rebellion on my part threatened the precarious balance he struggled to maintain and threw him into a rage.

Perhaps that's why my father was so quick to believe that David's seizures in church were evidence of demonic possession. "That boy's got something bad inside him," he said.

I imagine it must have been particularly difficult for my father to witness David's seizures; he knew what it was to be on display, and, though he had great empathy for those who suffered misfortunes they couldn't prevent—farmers who lost their crops to bad

weather, women whose husbands ran out on them—when he believed that someone was responsible for his own downfall, he was
less forgiving. "He better get himself right," he said about David.

One Saturday afternoon that summer some boys we knew were
out larking, riding a tractor down a gravel road and trying to set
the brake and spin the tractor around. It tipped over instead. One
boy was trapped beneath the tractor, his pelvis crushed.

That evening we went to the hospital and sat in the waiting
room with the injured boy's family and friends, waiting for news.
I felt shy, dumbstruck by the sudden proximity of death. My father said to the boy's uncle, Arthur, "I think it's all been worked
out—whatever it is that's meant to happen."

Arthur was a slender man who wore glasses with clear plastic
frames. He was polite and soft-spoken, with a grace and gentility
that was rare among famers in that part of the world. He seemed
better suited to be a teacher or a minister.

"A lot of folks," he said, "have been going down to the cha-
pel to pray."

My father was sitting across from him. He leaned forward and
tapped the point of his hook on Arthur's knee. I believe he meant it
as a kind gesture, but what he said next was anything but reassur-
ing. "Arthur, I reckon God laid all this out a good way back, and
there's nothing we can do but wait to see how it's going to end."

That was what my father believed: that our fates had been pre-
determined and were out of our hands. I imagine it helped him
come to terms with his own loss, and now he was offering his belief to Arthur as a comfort, having no idea that it was the last thing
a man who was waiting for word on whether his nephew would
live or die wanted to hear.

Although Arthur was too polite to speak sharply to my father,
I could tell from the way he drew back his head and pressed his

lips together that he was angry. He took off his glasses and held the bridge of his nose between two fingers as if he had a headache or perhaps a sharp pain in his eyes. There were white lines along both of his temples where his glasses had prevented the skin from tanning, and something about those white lines made him seem even sadder to me. I wished I could have said something to make up for my father's thoughtlessness, but I was just a boy, so I sat there, feeling the shame that my father should have felt.

"You didn't have to say that," my mother told him in the car on the drive home.

"I just told him what I think."

"You could have been more understanding." My mother turned and looked out her window at the distant lights of the farmhouses set far back from the highway. It would be a few days before we knew that the boy had made it through the worst and would be all right. "Mercy," my mother said. "That's what people need when they're in trouble." My father held his tongue, and the quiet settled around us, and I felt glad for my mother's soft voice, her compassion.

I remembered that night and my mother's words when a doctor in Texas said to me, "You poor soul."

Her name was Suzanne, and right away I thought of the Leonard Cohen song that goes: "Now Suzanne takes your hand / And she leads you to the river." I'd told her about my corneal erosions, which had continued in Texas, and she was the first doctor to react with empathy, as if she could truly imagine how horrible the past year had been for me.

All the same, she was a doctor, and after I'd told her about having a hyperactive thyroid gland when I was a teenager and the medicine that I'd taken, she said, "I wouldn't be surprised if you had an *under*active thyroid now. Almost everyone who's been treated for hyperthyroidism at some point develops hypothyroidism."

She explained that the medication I'd taken had worked by killing off a portion of my thyroid gland—probably too much of it. It was a safe bet that this was why my eyes were dry.

I mentioned Sjögren's syndrome, and she said, "Oh, sure. Could be. But let's test the thyroid first and see what happens. Okay?"

She had a round, pleasant face and a kind smile. She wore gray felt-covered clogs, green surgical scrubs, and a fuzzy sweater the color of apricots, its sleeves pushed up to her elbows. On one forefinger was a purple Bugs Bunny Band-Aid. It was that Band-Aid, more than anything else, that let me believe she wasn't just a doctor but a human being as well and that we were in this fight together. And I said to her what I'd been wanting to say to someone for a year. "Yes," I said. I told her, "Yes."

She turned out to be right: my thyroid gland was underactive. After a few months of oral medication, I was sleeping through the night, no longer awakened by horrible pain in my eyes.

As the years go on, I sometimes feel a gritty sensation, just enough of a scratch to remind me of my past agony. It happens most often in autumn or in spring, as it is now when I write this. But I can't bemoan the occasional twinge or itch or the fact that for the rest of my life I'll use liquid tears and ointment at night. I've made room for such minor annoyances, made up my mind to welcome them for what they are: a means of respecting health, of never forgetting suffering.

I still remember how David jerked and twitched those Sundays in church, how he fell to the floor, eyes closed, and slipped away into some world only he could know. At the time I gave no thought about what he brought back with him when he awoke, surrounded by those who loved him, but now I suspect it was something hard to describe, as it must have been for my father when he came home after his amputations, as it was for me when a corneal erosion would finally start to abate. I imagine that David felt inept. We, his friends and neighbors, had witnessed what the seizures did to his body, but how could he tell any of us what they did to his spirit?

Each time I saw David in church, I could tell that the seizures and the rumors about their cause were breaking him down. His previously erect posture—spine straight, shoulders back, chin lifted—had crumbled. He slouched and shuffled down the aisle to his pew and sat with his shoulders sagging, his head bowed. He no longer took part in the services, not trusting his body even to hold the weight of his Bible while he read to the congregation or to keep the Communion tray, with its dainty glasses, steady.

Now, after suffering through my own body's breakdown, I can imagine what he might have told us when he came back from a thrashing seizure had he been able to find the words: that he resented us just a little because we couldn't feel how worn-out he was with the constant and exhausting effort to be well. That he had come to both cherish and despise the memory of his vigor and strength. But, more than that, he surely loved us for what he knew: that we were all frail bodies, frail souls, all of us luminous in the light of health's grace, all of us happy to let that brightness blind us and keep our eyes from the shadows lurking behind, those specters of our impermanence, the ones that David, having come back from the darkness, could clearly see.

Such a Life

Summer 1982

I find the card in a drawer at my parents' house, a union card that
identifies my father as a member of the Amalgamated Association of Iron and Steel Workers, a fact that surprises me because
I've never heard him talk about this part of his life.

It was during the Great Depression, he tells me, when the bottom fell out of crop prices and he left the farm in southern Illinois and went north to East Chicago, where my uncle got him a
job at Inland Steel.

All my life I've watched him wear down his body working our
farm. He's wrestled with machinery, hefted hay bales, feed sacks,
wagon tongues, stock racks. He's spent days in the summer sun,
cultivating corn and beans, cutting wheat and hay. Winters, in
sub-zero weather, he's chopped ice at our pond and hauled water
to our hogs. I've seen his shoulders sag as he comes in from the
field, his boots shuffling through the dust as if he can barely lift

his feet. When I was young, I never really appreciated the work he did. Although I would come to feel the same strain and weariness in my own body days I spent riding a tractor or later working in factories, I always thought it something I would one day escape. Like my mother, who taught grade school, I was in love with books, and, as I grew into my early adult years, I set my sights on how far away from farms and factories my imagination and words could take me.

My father sits slumped in his chair, his face weathered, the skin loose on his neck. He's sixty-nine years old. "Now that was work," he says to me. "That steel. That was damned hard work."

Summer 1894

A current of red fire—molten metal—spills over the edge of a platform at the Homestead Mill near Pittsburgh and falls on the head and back of a worker. When the other workers cut his burned clothing from him, his flesh peels away in strips.

Summer 2003

There are men who make their fortunes on the backs of people like my father, and the industrialist Henry Clay Frick was one of them. I can't help but be aware of that fact the first time I step into Frick's mansion, Clayton, come to Pittsburgh on the invitation of the Frick Historical Center as a guest artist. My assignment is to respond to Frick's life with a piece of writing.

To be honest, it's an assignment for which I fear I'm a poor match because, when it comes to affluence, I've never been one of the "haves." In fact, I've always been leery of money made from commerce—just a tad resentful—and now what I already know about Frick irritates me. He acquired his wealth by cooking coal long enough to burn off the impurities—sulfur and phosphorous—thereby creating coke, a pure-carbon form of coal that produced the sort of intense heat needed for making steel. In 1882, when Frick was thirty-three, he entered into a partnership with the steel baron Andrew Carnegie. Notoriously antilabor, Frick was overseeing Carnegie's Homestead Steel Mill in 1892 when the workers staged a wildcat strike and Frick's decision to bring in Pinkerton guards led to violence. Before that, in 1878, he was one of the investors who acquired an abandoned canal reservoir in the Allegheny Mountains forty miles northwest of Pittsburgh, a spot that would become the South Fork Fishing and Hunting Club, a playground and retreat for the upper class.

Located 450 feet above Johnstown, the club had its own lake, created with a large earthen dam. It was the largest man-made lake in the world, covering more than seven hundred acres and containing twenty million tons of water. Because of a series of engineering faults, not to mention a leveling of the top of the dam to allow club members the width necessary for carriages to have two-way traffic lanes, the dam gave way on Memorial Day 1889 and sent all that water rushing through the Conemaugh Gorge and onto the people of Johnstown. Ten thousand people died in the flood and the ensuing fires from oil tanks rupturing and bursting into an inferno of flames.

So there's the Johnstown Flood, the Homestead Steel strike, and the year before it the riots at Frick's Morewood Mine and Coke Works, where his guards shot and killed eleven strikers. All incidents in which the working class suffered for the sake of Frick's wealth and leisure.

Now, over a hundred years later, I step into his home, feeling a great divide between us, a gap of not just time but, more important, one of economics and social class. I can't help but think of my ancestors who built their log cabins in Washington County, just south of Pittsburgh, and then began migrating west in search of better land. I can't get out of my head the fact that our modest frame farmhouse in southern Illinois had no indoor plumbing, that we used chamber pots at night and emptied them each morning at the outdoor privy. I know if, by some quirk of fate, my father and Henry Clay Frick had lived at the same time, Frick would have been the sort of man my father would have looked at with contempt. "That Frick," I can hear my father saying from the grave. "He thinks his shit don't stink."

Such a glitter show, this Clayton, located in the East End of Pittsburgh at the corner of Penn and Homewood avenues. Purchased in 1882 as a belated wedding present for Frick's wife, Adelaide, the Italianate house originally consisted of two stories and eleven rooms. Clay and Ada moved into the home in 1883, after Frick had given the renowned Pittsburgh architect Andrew Peebles a year to make renovations. During that time Clay and Ada made trips to New York to purchase furniture and draperies and artwork. Eight years later Frick again hired an architect—this time Frederick J. Osterling—to add a third and fourth story to Clayton and to increase its number of rooms to twenty-four.

This is the house I step into on a summer morning. Clayton has been open for public tours since 1990, and indeed one of the docents is ushering a group of schoolchildren through the music conservatory as I arrive with my personal guide, Robin Pflasterer, Clayton's registrar. Robin is a pleasant, sweet-voiced woman who knows a good deal about the Fricks and the turn-of-the-century Victorian society they embraced and upheld at Clayton. She moves with a very confident manner, her posture straight but not rigid, her head up but not haughty. It's clear that she's at home here, and why shouldn't she be, since she's the one responsible for seeing that Clayton is "dressed" according to the season? Here in

summer the woolen carpets have been taken up and sisal matting
is on the floor; slipcovers are on the sofas and chairs, as would
have been the case when the Fricks lived here and wanted to protect the furniture from the mill soot that would have drifted in
through the open windows.

Robin says hello to one of the security guards, a woman in a
navy blazer and gray slacks. The guard wears white gloves to protect whatever she has to touch during the hours of her duties. I
understand that I have just entered a "don't touch" world where
I am to feel privileged to be in the midst of opulence.

"We called ahead," Robin says. "They said it would be all right
to take photographs."

My camera hangs from its strap around my neck. Not just
anyone would be allowed to take photos inside Clayton. I don't
know who "they" are, but apparently I have "them" to thank for
approving my request. The guard studies me then nods her head
and steps to the side. I follow Robin, understanding that I have
been given special dispensation and that in Robin's company I
am free to roam about Clayton, even invited to go beyond the velvet rope that closes off the fourth floor, where Frick artifacts have
been cataloged and stored. At one point Robin opens a window,
and we step out onto the roof, the same roof where the Fricks'
daughter Helen and her friends often climbed to the highest spot.

I'm reminded of Big Daddy in Tennessee Williams's *Cat on a
Hot Tin Roof* and how he liked to go up on the widow's walk atop
his plantation manor and gaze out at the richest land in all of the
Mississippi Delta, acres and acres as far as the eye could see and
all of it belonging to him.

Dare I admit to a similar feeling of propriety as I stand on the
Clayton roof, where ordinary visitors never stand? It pains me
to confess that as much as I'm resisting Frick's wealth and the

way it bought him separation from the working class—protection from people like my own family—I'm also seduced by the special privilege that allows me to stand on the top of this grand mansion and look down on the heads of another tour group, just now passing beneath me.

Once, at Marina Towers in downtown Chicago, I stood on a thirty-fifth-floor terrace and poured water from an ice bucket over the railing. The height was so great that the water evaporated before it could reach the street. What a feeling, to watch that water come apart, sparkling an instant in the sunlight, before vanishing as if some miserly hand from above had reached down and snatched it out of the air.

Summer 1902

Teddy Roosevelt is coming to Clayton. A Fourth of July luncheon. John Philip Sousa and his orchestra are to provide the music, and, the evening before, Frick gets the fidgets about it all, worried that something will go wrong.

He strolls through Clayton, his daughter Helen accompanying him as she often does when he's restless and can't sit still. She links her arm in his—Helen, the second daughter, the one who was only three when her "Tissie," Martha, died at the age of six. Helen is beginning to grow out of her girlhood; she is fourteen and well aware that her father will always dote on her as if she's a child because to him she will always represent some memory of Martha.

Just tonight, as he was reading in the library, Papsie pulled her down onto his lap and said, "There you are, Dove. There's my wee Dolly." Talking a father's baby talk.

Helen has seen him, when he didn't know anyone was watching, lean over and kiss Martha's high chair, which still sits in the breakfast room as if one morning Helen and her brother, Childs, will come downstairs and there she'll be. Papsie has a curl of Martha's red hair that he keeps in a box in the drawer of his bureau, and sometimes he shows it to Helen, and together they kiss it, their lips so close together.

Tonight Helen says, "I'd give President Roosevelt a gift. A painting. That's what I'd give him, Papsie."

He's fallen in love with the baby talk. "Oh, oo would, would oo, Dolly?"

"The Chartran," Helen says. "The one you commissioned to commemorate the end of the Spanish-American War. Wouldn't President Roosevelt love that one ever so much?"

"I expect you're right, Dolly." He pats her hand. "You're no slouch."

They take their time climbing the stairs. Below them the orchestrion—its collection of drums and cymbals and brass and woodwinds—is playing the overture from Friedrich von Flotow's opera *Martha*, and Frick stops and sings to "The Last Rose of Summer":

I love in a dream,
A dream that never dies.
I hear her gentle voice.
I see her lovely eyes.

Upstairs, in Helen's room, a garden mural adorns the walls: white roses, chrysanthemums, and wisteria. Hummingbirds, bluebirds, and butterflies flit about clouds on the ceiling. On the east wall between two windows that look out over the garden, a single rosebud, the family's nickname for Martha, is separate from the others and the only one that is reddish pink. It looks as if it's falling, its bud tilted down.

"She was a lovely little creature," Frick says with a sigh. "Your sister." He draws Helen closer to him, pats her hand, leans over to give her a kiss.

Summer 2003

As I follow Robin from room to room—the solarium; the parlor; the reception room; the scullery; the breakfast room; the library; the children's playroom; Frick's bedroom and across the hall, Adelaide's (Robin tells me that some nights Frick would tap on Adelaide's door and she would permit him to come in to "pay a visit"), I take in the gleaming walls of mahogany and walnut and oak where paintings by artists such as Jean-François Millet, Jules-Adolphe Breton, and Johannes Vermeer, all acquired with Frick's money, hang. The ceilings are aluminum leaf. The windows have fourteen-carat gold handles.

I can hardly imagine the sort of life that went on at Clayton— the luxury and the leisure—while in the mills men were losing fingers and toes or, worse, their lives, all for the sake of what the Slav workers called "za chlebom," their right to their daily bread.

After Roosevelt's luncheon that Fourth of July in 1902, the president stretched out for a nap on a chaise lounge in the "Blue Room," where Adelaide's sister, Martha, had often stayed.

In our farmhouse we propped up our windows with the sawed-off ends of broomsticks. On our plaster walls two paintings hung: one of Jesus kneeling in the Garden of Gethsemane on the night of his betrayal; the other a landscape of a snow-capped mountain rising up behind a blue lake.

I chuckle when I read in Helen's memoir that her mother was "a meticulous housekeeper." So easy to be meticulous, I think, when the lady of the house has three maids, a butler-valet, a cook, and a nursemaid and a governess for the children. Helen also recalls that her mother was always kept so busy cleaning and arranging things. Well, I suppose that's the way it goes (even if I can take Helen at her word and imagine Adelaide engaged in physical labor) when you have all those rooms, all that woodwork, all that glitz. Someone has to keep it clean of the soot drifting in the windows, the grime produced by the mills that make the millions that buy such a house as Clayton.

Summer 1969

The house in town—the one my parents eventually buy instead of remodeling our farmhouse, where the roof is leaking, plaster is flaking from the walls, and we still have no indoor plumbing— has three bedrooms, a living room, a dining room, a kitchen, and a bathroom. My parents buy it for ten thousand dollars.

The man who sells it to us is a welder, and evenings and weekends he's remodeled the house. The floors are made of hardwood. The walls in the living room and dining room have paneling on them. We have a bathtub and a toilet. In the kitchen there are wrought iron rods running from the undersides of the cabinets to the countertop. Screwed into the rods are iron circles where my mother can set flowerpots. She traces her finger around those hoops the first time she sees them. "Now that's fancy," she says. Such are the limits of our extravagance.

Summer 2003

My wife and I live in Columbus, Ohio, on a cul-de-sac, a term I still think sounds more highfalutin than what it really is: a dead-end street. Our house is nearly identical to the others, one of the two or three models the builders put up in the late 1980s: two-story box houses with aluminum siding, a smattering of brick or stone here and there, two-car garages, basements, decks. We have

a little over two thousand square feet of living space, and still
sometimes I drive down Dublin Road or Riverside Drive, where
the million-dollar houses sit on the banks of the Scioto—houses
with gates to the driveways; houses with outdoor tennis courts,
indoor swimming pools, landscaped steps leading down to boat
docks—and, even though I don't play tennis, have never learned
to swim, can't imagine any use I'd ever have for a boat, for just a
moment I envy the people who live in those houses, not so much
for what they own but for everything that I don't.

It's silly, really—downright shameful—to feel this way because in truth my wife and I are comfortable. I suppose you'd say
we're middle-class. We don't lack in spite of how we gripe sometimes about my teacher's salary, our only income, or how we say,
"Oh, if we just had this" or "Oh, if we just had that." We should
be content. We have money in the bank—not a Frick fortune, to
be sure, but money all the same for a rainy day.

In the winter a local grocery chain was going out of business,
closing down its stores. In the most bitter cold of January I saw
people standing along this same street in front of one of the stores,
holding signs advertising the store's liquidation. How many hours,
I wondered, did they have to stand there, beaten numb by the
wind, and what were they able to do with the money they made?

The summer after I graduated with my master's degree in English, I worked a series of odd jobs to make ends meet. I rode my bicycle to Hardee's and cooked burgers. I walked the streets compil-
ing a pre-census enumeration list at twenty-five cents an address.
I umpired slow-pitch softball games in the city recreation league
and let grown men curse at me. One day I went to a training ses-
sion for people who wanted to sell Rainbow Vacuum Cleaners.
The people in charge gave us a standard pitch to use while trying
to make a sale, and we spent the morning practicing. I watched

middle-aged men, who for whatever reasons were out of work and desperate for this job, stumble over lines such as "You might ask yourself what is this amazing item? Is it the world's biggest roll-on deodorant, or is it R2-D2 from *Star Wars*? No, it's the marvelous Rainbow." The men stammered and started over. They hemmed and hawed and cleared their throats and said, man, there was a lot to remember, wasn't there? "But you," one of them said to me. "You're a natural. Slick, you got a way with words."

Summer 2003

As we stroll through Clayton, Robin tells me that Frick's mother was the daughter of Abraham Overholt, owner of a distillery in West Overton, Pennsylvania. Frick's father was a miller in that distillery, and Overholt wasn't particularly pleased when he found out that this red-haired rowdy Frick had impregnated his daughter. A wedding of necessity took place, and Overholt allowed a single act of charity; he let the newly married couple live in the spring house that sat only a few yards away from the manor. There the first child, Maria, was born, and a year later the first son, Henry Clay Frick, came into the world in that tiny two-room house, springwater running beneath it.

When Robin tells me this fact and goes on to point out some of the earliest paintings that Frick acquired—Troyon's *A Pasture in Normandy*, Cuyp's *Cows and Herdsman by a River*—I have to adjust my thinking because I, too, come from a land of pastures and cattle. When I drive away from Columbus now and find myself suddenly out in the open, as I did this past weekend, traveling across southern Indiana farmland on my way to teach at a writers' conference in New Harmony, I feel my body relax, my heart unclench, and I'm content to follow the blacktop road that spurs off from the interstate and winds along fields where wheat is turning golden, nearly ready to cut. I slow for each bend and curve, in no hurry, falling into the rhythm of the terrain, a landscape a colleague who didn't know that landscape was mine described as particularly ugly. But to me it's all lovely—the fields, the farmhouses sitting off the road down lanes, the whitewashed fences, the way land stretches off to the horizon, and, above, the graceful glide of hawks circling in the air. It's lovely for its openness, its lack of clutter, its simplicity. Here is the creek, the pasture, the sky. I want to take all this inside me and carry it back to the city.

Standing in Clayton, looking at those paintings of country villages and working people sowing grain, bringing in the harvest, caring for cattle and sheep, I can't help but wonder how many times Frick wished he could trade the mansion and all its finery for that two-room springhouse and the soothing sound of water.

Lord knows he had trouble aplenty. His darling Martha died in 1891, after a four-year wasting illness. The following year another baby, Henry Clay Frick Jr., lived only a little more than a month, dying on August 3, 1892. Frick's millions couldn't buy him protection against sorrow. After the second child's death, a rumor sprang up in a newspaper item that someone was trying to poison the Fricks. Given the unrest at the Homestead mill and Frick's history of animosity toward labor unions, it isn't a stretch to imagine that he lived uneasily in his fine Clayton. Not that he would ever admit it. Always the stoic, he turned a defiant face toward those who would wish him harm.

Here in Clayton, however, the signs of how deeply he was capable of feeling are everywhere. In the library Robin points out the checkbook open on the desk, each check containing an image of Martha, Frick's darling. What a poignant pairing of the divided sensibilities of this man—his materialism and his sentimentality. In the reception room a life-sized bust of Martha rests on an elaborate pedestal in front of a window, sheer lace curtains filtering the light into a soft glow that seems to emanate from the child. Frick commissioned a Roman sculptor, Orazio Andreoni, to create the bust. Martha's arms are folded and resting on a cloud as if she looks at visitors from a spot in heaven.

"Mr. Frick idealized Martha after her death," Robin tells me. "Her presence is everywhere in Clayton."

Frick commissioned Théobald Chartran to paint a posthumous portrait of Martha in 1895, a portrait that hangs in Frick's bedroom. Chartran restored Martha's auburn curls, the luxurious hair that had fallen out during her long illness. He wreathed her torso in flowers: narcissus, buttercups, poppies, and forget-me-nots.

What sorrow must have filled Clayton in the days following the children's deaths, a grief Frick maintained and at the same time tried to assuage through the artwork he collected. In the dining room, on the wall directly across from where he sat each evening for his dinner, is Pascal-Adolphe-Jean Dagnan-Bouveret's *Consolatrix Afflictorum*, a painting measuring 7'3" x 6'4". The Madonna sits in a wooded glade, the Christ child on her lap. Hummingbirds flutter around them, while behind three angels are playing music. One of them plucks a harp, another bows a violin, and the third strums a lute. At the Madonna's feet a nearly naked man lies prostrate with grief, his hand covering his face.

So it must have seemed for Frick once he knew that his wealth couldn't stop trouble from finding him.

Summer 1892

The anarchist Alexander Berkman, lover of Emma Goldman, bursts into Frick's downtown Pittsburgh office. Frick is sitting at his desk, his back to the door, conducting business with John G. A. Leishman, the vice president of Carnegie Steel.

Berkman raises a revolver. "Frick," he says, and Frick turns in his swivel chair.

A brilliant light streams through the window that Berkman faces. It's nearly two o'clock on a Saturday afternoon, July 23. Berkman fires, and there's a bright flash from the revolver. Frick cries out in pain as the bullet enters his neck at the base of the skull and lodges in the middle of his back. Leishman leaps to his feet and grabs Berkman.

Berkman fires again. This time the bullet pierces the right side of Frick's neck. Still, the wounds aren't fatal, and, as Berkman struggles to escape Leishman's grasp, he fires a third time. The bullet misses Frick completely and strikes the wall behind him.

By this time a carpenter working in the building has come into the office and is striking Berkman on the head with his hammer. Berkman drops his revolver but manages to take a dagger from his pocket and stab Frick in his back, his hip, his right side, and his left leg before deputy sheriffs arrive.

A summons goes out for Dr. J. J. Buchanan, whose office is nearby. When he arrives, Frick refuses anesthesia. He wants to be awake, he says, to better help Buchanan feel his way to the bullets.

Buchanan quickly locates the first, probing while Frick sits in his chair. The second takes him two hours to find. "There, that feels like it," Frick finally says.

Berkman has gashed Frick's leg so deeply that the tendons have almost been severed. Once Buchanan has dressed all the wounds, Frick insists on staying to finish the day's business. He signs letters, completes the details for a loan deal, and finally sends a telegram to his mother. "Was shot twice," he tells her, "but not dangerously."

At Clayton, Adelaide is still recovering from delivering Henry Clay Frick Jr. This Saturday is the first day she's been out of bed since the birth. Her sister, Attie, is the one who tells her that Clay has been shot. "Only a superficial wound," Attie says. "Nothing to worry about, Ada dear."

At eight o'clock that night four men carry Frick up the stairs at Clayton on an iron cot. Adelaide is in bed, behind the closed door of her room, and, when she hears the commotion on the stairs, she calls out for Clay.

Frick says in a casual tone. "Ada, I'll be in to see you as soon as I get washed and cleaned up."

Later Attie and her brother Marshall lift Adelaide from her bed to a rocking chair. They pull the chair across the hall to Frick's bedroom and gently put her into bed beside him. Both of them sedated, they drift off to sleep, and that's how the day of the assassination attempt ends, husband and wife who ordinarily spend each night in separate beds—who have lost one child and will soon lose another—sleeping in this grand home I'll move through 111 summers later, taking note of the framed photograph on Frick's dressing table, a photograph of Adelaide and Childs and Martha that would have been there that night in 1892. Along the bottom, in Frick's backward slanting handwriting, is the inscription "My Jewels."

Autumn 1979

My father is sixty-six years old. He's worn down his body doing damned hard work, as he'll one day say of his time in the steel mill, damned hard work like the work he's done on our eighty acres.

I'm living away from home. I'm married and working my first job after graduating from college. "A pencil-pusher's job," my father calls it. I coordinate an educational outreach program that helps economically or culturally disadvantaged young people get into college. I start the job in September, and through the autumn, while my father is harvesting soybeans, I'm at my desk or out in "the field," identifying potential clients.

The farm and the shoulder-to-the-grindstone work it takes has never appealed to me, and I don't for a minute think that I'm disappointing my father by turning away from it. Although he's proud of me and the life I'm making for myself, one day I'll imagine that a part of him wished that I was working alongside him those last years he farmed our ground. But I'm not thinking such things in 1979. I'm too busy starting my adult life.

I'm living in Evansville, Indiana, eighty miles away from home, and, though my mother writes letters that autumn with news of the harvest, I rarely give a second thought to what it takes for my sixty-six-year-old father to keep straining his muscles and heart with work.

On occasion I have to drive to Vincennes for meetings, and at the end of the day I cross the bridge into Illinois and travel twenty miles more to my parents' house. If a meeting is on a Friday or a Monday, my wife comes with me, and we spend the weekend with my mother and father.

These autumn days he slithers beneath his combine each morning to grease the fittings, forcing his heavy body into tight spaces. His toe joints ache from gout, so he gingerly places a foot on the tractor's drawbar and pulls himself up onto the seat. That International M bounces over the rutted fields, jostling him. He has to keep getting down from the tractor whenever he has a hopper full of beans, to empty it into the bed of his truck. Then he has to climb back on the M again and start another series of passes around the field.

He wears narrow-toed boots, and his toe throbs inside them each time he pulls himself up onto the M, each time he walks over the rough ground. He doesn't think about stopping; that isn't a possibility. It's harvest time, and, as he has done so many years, he has a crop to bring in. It doesn't matter how he feels. He can rest come winter. That's what he always says. Plenty of rest come winter.

Then one Monday evening, when my meeting in Vincennes is over, I come back to my parents' house, where my wife is waiting. We'll have supper here and then drive back to Evansville.

It surprises me to see my father's truck parked in the driveway since there's still daylight left, and I can't imagine why he hasn't used every bit of it before pulling the tractor and combine into the machine shed and calling it quits for the day.

"Your dad's not feeling well," my mother tells me.

He's in bed, rolled over on his side with his back to me. "I'm sick," he says when I ask him what's wrong.

We've reached a point in our relationship, that point that men so often reach, where the only way we can show each other affection is through good-natured teasing.

"Sick?" I say. "What do you mean you're sick? You sure you're not just goldbricking?"

"I'm sick to my stomach." His voice is as flat, as weary, as I've ever heard it, and I can tell from its sound that indeed something is ailing him. "I've been sick all afternoon."

"Do you want to go to the doctor?" I'm ready to take him, ready to help him to the car and drive him to the hospital, ready to call for an ambulance if that's what we need. "Don't you think you should?"

"I've just got an upset stomach," he says.

But it isn't just an upset stomach. It is, as my mother tells me when she calls me in Evansville late the next evening, a heart attack, his first. He worked that afternoon with the pressure in his chest. He threw up in the field and kept working. He broke out in a cold sweat and still kept working. It took him the rest of the day and that night and most of the next day finally to admit he was in trouble.

"If you'd waited any longer," the doctor tells him, "you'd have ended up dead."

Three years later he'll be mowing the yard on one of the hottest days of the summer and his heart will give out for good. That's what work does to a man. At least the kind of work my father did. Breaks him down. Kills him.

Summer 2003

Surely Frick knew that about the work the men did in his mills. How could he not? Still, he fought their unions, locked them out, called in Pinkerton guards. Shortly after Berkman's attempted assassination, a mediator tried to resolve the Homestead strike. The mediator came to Frick's bedroom at Clayton and outlined the striking workers' final terms.

Frick's face was ashen, recovering as he was from Berkman's wounds, but still his voice was firm and strong. He wouldn't give in, he told the mediator. "If it takes all summer and all winter and all next summer and next winter," he said. "Yes, even my life itself. I will fight this thing to the bitter end. I will never recognize the Union, never, never!"

As we stand now in the same bedroom, Robin tells me about a photograph the archivists took of one of Frick's vests just for the purpose of documenting it. Since no one is wearing it, the vest is flat and empty, and by some trick of light a shadow falls just above where Frick's heart would have been.

"I've always carried that impression with me," she says.

We're standing beside Frick's bed, and I'm looking at his slippers on the floor in front of the night table, slippers that are cu-

riously feminine, with their gold-thread stitching and their em-
broidery of red and white flowers. On the wall above the night
table, within easy reach of Frick as he lay in bed, is a row of six
buttons, each of them ready to sound a chime somewhere else
in the house and summon a valet, a maid, a butler, a nurse, a
coachman, even Mrs. Frick across the hall in her own bedroom—
everyone within easy reach of the man whose millions bought
and renovated this elaborate home.

Such a life of ease. Anything you want, yours. Anything except
your daughter Martha, dead, or your son Henry Clay Jr., dead.
No amount of money, not even the sort of fortune that Frick had,
could buy them back.

All through Clayton his grief mixes with his wealth, and I imagine if the ghosts of Johnstown, Morewood, Homestead, could
drift through these rooms, rub over the mahogany and walnut
and oak woodwork, the parquet floors, the aluminum leaf ceilings, the satin wallpaper, the chandeliers, the stained glass, the
marble bust of Martha, the rosebud mural on Helen's bedroom
wall, the *Consolatrix Afflictorum*, they would call such beautiful
anguish right and fair, gathered as it was from misery, from the
danger the mill workers faced, the risks they took, and all they
asked from muscle and nerve and bone.

Such a life, I would say to my father if I could, as I didn't that
evening when he lay in his bed, his heart seized in his chest. Such
a life of toil. All our straining. Such a life of work.

Twan't Much

At the tire repairs factory I knew a man named Jack, who had no teeth, who brought the same thing for lunch every day, a fried egg sandwich in a wrinkled and stained paper bag. He had a family he could barely support, one that didn't have, as my father often said, "as much as a pot to piss in." This was in 1976, a time of double-digit inflation and high interest rates in a small midwestern town going nowhere fast.

One day, Friday the week of Christmas, I brought Jack a platter of homemade cookies. I gave it to him in the parking lot after work. "For you and your family," I said, certain he'd be pleased.

I was twenty-one and saving money to go back to college. I had no idea that my gift would call attention to the fact that Jack's life would more than likely always be exactly what it was at that moment. He was a poor man with poor prospects.

He bowed his head. He held that platter in his big hands, callused and scarred, the knuckles all knobbed up, and he mumbled,

"Much obliged." Then he walked away, leaving me to feel the embarrassment I'd caused him, the shame.

The next day my wife and I found a box of Whitman's Chocolates leaning against our front door. No card. No note of explanation. But I knew right away that Jack had left them for us.

The factory held its Christmas party at the Elks Lodge that evening, and I watched him get drunk on free liquor, so drunk that toward the end of the evening he was sick outside the bathroom and his wife had to ask for help hauling him to the car.

Come Monday he was back at work, cutting slabs of rubber from the mill drum. I never said a word to him about those Whitman's Chocolates, nor did I tell him that I wished that I or someone else had told him to lay off the booze that night at the party, to let him know he didn't need to ruin what was a fine evening for his wife—a prime rib dinner, a few spins around the dance floor—and that was sure as heck what he was going to do if he kept guzzling that bourbon. How in the hell would you say that to a man ground down by work and the circumstances of his life on a night when he had a chance to cut loose, when the liquor was free and, for at least a little while, so was he?

Well, you don't say it. That's what. I regretted the gift of the cookies and all it had wrought, so I kept my yap shut.

Then the day comes when I'm back in college, and I'm in a theater class, and one day I'm performing in a scene from *Our Town*. It's the scene at the end of the play when the Webbs' daughter, Emily, is granted her wish to come back from the dead and relive one day of her life. She chooses her twelfth birthday. February 11, 1899.

I play Constable Warren, who meets up with Emily's father, the newspaper editor, outside on the street as he's coming home from the train station. My character has been out early to rescue a drunk, asleep in a snowdrift near Polish Town. Constable

Warren has been doing his work on a morning when it's ten degrees below zero. He's saved a man's life, but still he doesn't mean much of anything to the give-and-take of the Webb family that morning. He's just a minor character, a simple man of duty, on the periphery of their lives.

I have a line at the end of the scene, a line I've worked over and over, trying to get it to please me. Constable Warren, when Mr. Webb says he'll have to put word of that rescue up near Polish Town in the newspaper, says, "Twan't much." I want just the right balance of humility and pride and unease. Just the right hint of things unsaid, things I learned from a work-worn man one Christmas season when neither of us knew that he had anything to teach me.

"Twan't much," I say.

The next thing is easy. The exit. All I have to do is leave.

Election Season

The man on the corner, Ed, has a snowblower, and all winter, whenever we get a fresh accumulation, he cleans out his driveway and then the sidewalk as far as my own drive, three houses down the cul-de-sac. I don't know him very well, but, when I watch him clearing my sidewalk, I think of my father, who taught me the kind gestures between neighbors that take so little effort and make everyone a bit more cozy.

Summers, my wife and I return the favor of the snow blowing by sharing tomatoes from our garden with Ed and his wife, Cindy. We live with only one house between us, and yet we know so little about one another. They know I teach at Ohio State, that we grow heirloom tomatoes in our garden; we know that Ed has a snowblower and he's happy to put it to use so we'll have a clean sidewalk. When I see him out in the cold, doing something he doesn't have to for people he barely knows, I think there goes a good neighbor.

Then, one glorious Sunday in early autumn, he knocks on

our front door. He has a clipboard in his hand, a big smile on his meaty face.

"Hot for this time of year, isn't it?" he says to my wife. "Darned hot." He hands Deb a small sandwich bag with a few Brach's candies inside—cinnamon, peppermint, butterscotch, toffee—and a slip of paper that says, *Bless the Family: Save the Nation.* "Election Day's coming," he says. "You've heard about Issue 1?"

Issue 1 is the proposed amendment to the Ohio state constitution that, if passed, will make marriage between a man and a woman the only union that the state will legally recognize. It's the "antigay" amendment, and Ed is at our house to get our signatures on a petition to put Issue 1 on the November ballot.

"I'm sorry," Deb tells him. "I can't sign."

Ed's confused. His eyebrows go up. He gives Deb a tentative grin. "But you're married, aren't you?"

"My husband and I have an open mind about this sort of thing."

Ed pulls his head back. His eyes narrow. "Oh," he says. "I see. Well, that's too bad."

It isn't long before almost every front lawn in our neighborhood sports a Bush-Cheney sign. Only one or two Kerrey-Edwards signs interrupt the Republican majority. Then there are lawns like ours that announce nothing at all. Let'em wonder, I think. Or, better yet, let 'em ask Ed.

When it comes to politics, I'm my father's son through and through—a Democrat—but even that affiliation makes me uneasy since, as my father said of most politicians, whether Democrat or Republican, "I wouldn't trust any of the bastards as far as I could throw 'em."

I pretty much feel the same. In fact, I don't even think of myself as a political person. Every four years I threaten not to vote.

Then, when it comes time, and the thought of a Republican in the White House presents itself, I knuckle down and do my duty. I march into that voting booth and vote for every Dem on the ballot.

My father was a Democrat because he was a child of the Depression who grew up on a farm in southern Illinois and blamed Herbert Hoover for everything. Hoobert Heever, he called him. Don't ask me why.

A Roosevelt Democrat, that was my father. He was working-class. He was the little guy. Republicans were out to protect the fat cats, he said, and he was never one of those.

Still, I suspect that, if he were alive today, he'd agree with Ed. He'd sign that petition in a whipstitch because toward the end of his life he was a Christian man who believed strongly in morality and was quite willing to let his church, the fundamentalist Church of Christ, define for him exactly what was moral and what wasn't. He objected to single men and women "shacking up." I'm fairly certain he never would have approved of a gay or lesbian marriage.

My mother was a timid, discreet woman who never discussed her politics. We all knew, though, that she voted Republican as her parents and her siblings had as long as memory could recall. That fact flummoxes me every time I think about it because my mother's family, the Reads, were little people just like the Martins. In fact, they may have been just a tad worse off than my father's family. The theory that people always vote their pocketbooks—the wealthy voting Republican and the poor voting Democratic—goes right out the window when it comes to the Reads. I have no idea how it came to be that they cast their lot with the Republicans, and I can't bring myself to ask my one surviving uncle because I fear it would lead to dissension the way it did a few years back during the Clinton versus Dole election, when his daughter confessed that she'd voted for Clinton, and my uncle said to her in a horrified voice, "Why, Melanie Ann. Your mother and I thought we raised you better than that."

From time to time now my wife says to me, "I couldn't have married you if you'd been a Republican." She wonders how partners of different political affiliations sustain a relationship.

"My mother and father did," I remind her.

"Your mother never talked about politics. She just let your dad blow."

That's true. I can recall my father and my uncle Bill Heath, who was married to my dad's sister, sitting on porches and around kitchen tables complaining about crop prices and farm subsidy programs and grain embargoes, and kicking the Republicans all to hell. My mother never said a word. She refilled iced tea glasses, served chiffon cakes, and kept everything she believed to herself.

In many ways I'm like my mother, unwilling to make my political beliefs public. How unfair it is, then, for me to spy a Republican sign on a neighbor's lawn and immediately feel a distaste for that person I may have only previously known as the driver of the Acura SUV or the one who has the ChemLawn service or who relies on Merry Maids for housecleaning (gee, it strikes me now that even those details are political—we carry our politics with us in the things we own, the services we engage, the stores we frequent; nothing is pure, not even the organic fertilizer I spread on our lawn). Who am I to pass judgment on these neighbors who profess their support for Bush-Cheney when I don't have the conviction to make my own pronouncement? I'm the guy who on late-night walks is tempted to rip out those Bush-Cheney signs, every last one of them. That's who I am. That guy.

When someone speaks of the Midwest, I think of small towns and farming communities like the ones in southern Illinois, where I grew up, and not the cities like Columbus, where I now live. To me the Midwest will always mean the countryside and the people who inhabit it. When I'm back in southern Illinois, as I am each summer, I like nothing more than to drive out into the country through the township where my father's farm now belongs to another man. I like to watch the fields of timothy grass ripple out toward a distant tree line when the wind comes up. I like the way the land is marked off into square sections, the gravel roads running at right angles. The straight rows of corn and soybeans, so neat and orderly, are beautiful. I can pull off the road at one of the graveyards where my ancestors are buried and for awhile hear nothing but the wind moving through the trees, a squirrel scrabbling through the grass, a crow calling from overhead, a bobwhite's two-note whistle. I like the farmhouses with their neatly tended gardens and their lawn ornaments—shiny gazing balls, carved wooden ducks with wings that circle with the wind, statues of deer and geese. Sometimes I'll see a collection of metal lawn chairs under the shade trees or a glider in a breezeway, and I'll know that come evening folks will gather there and for an hour or so their lives will be that simple—the gentle motion of the glider, the easy rock of the lawn chairs, the sun setting on another day of labor. Maybe someone will talk of the war in Iraq or what Bush is doing to squeeze the farmer or the price of gasoline, but eventually the voices will fade away, and the world will exist the way it did before politics. Twilight will give way to dusk, and the fireflies will come out. Bullfrogs will croak from the pond in the pasture. The bright stars will twinkle overhead, and the earth will keep turning over, despite our own stupidity and everything we do to threaten it.

My first political memory is the 1960 Kennedy-Nixon election. I was five years old, and I remember being in our car along a gravel road outside a church that was the polling place for my parents. A man came up to the car and offered me an apple. It was a yellow delicious—firm and sweet—and I remember how good it tasted on that sunny November day. Indian summer was lingering that year, and everything seemed to have a golden tone: the apple, the dried cornstalks, the yellow leaves on the hickory trees. How wonderful, I thought, this thing my parents called an election.

My father was in the car with me—babysitting, I suppose, while my mother was in the church casting her vote. He knew the man who gave me the apple. I remember that much. "Tell him thank you," my father said, and I did.

Of course, everyone knew everyone else in Lukin Township, and, once the election was done, they went back to their ordinary lives—the farmers and the schoolteachers and the oil field workers and the shop clerks. Summers, they helped each other bring in the hay; winters, they gathered around the radio at the Berryville General Store to listen to high school basketball games or went to each other's houses to play euchre or pitch. They might disagree about Kennedy, but in the end they were still these people in this township finding a way to get on with the living that had to be done there.

From time to time at harvest season a farmer got down on his luck—maybe he got hurt in an accident, or maybe he got sick and was laid up in bed—and then the other farmers in the township pulled together and brought in that man's crop. They brought their machinery, and they got the job done, no matter what their politics were. The season and the wheat or corn or beans in the fields didn't care about politics, and these men couldn't afford to either. At such times it didn't matter a whit who was a Republican and who was a Democrat.

I like to think, then, that there are certain things we hold in common here in the Midwest—a sense of fairness, a work ethic, a responsibility to our neighbors—but I have to admit that after Ed makes his appearance with his petition and the election season begins to percolate, I start to get testy.

"Republicans," I mutter when Deb and I are out for a walk and we pass the lawns with their Bush-Cheney signs on display.

Deb is even more agitated, vowing to withhold tomatoes from our Republican neighbors.

That'll teach 'em, I think. No Moonglows or Lemon Boys or Black Russians for you or you or you.

It turns out that the young man who lives in the house between ours and Ed's puts a Bush-Cheney sign in his yard. If he's on his porch or in his driveway as we go past in our car, Deb keeps her eyes straight ahead. "Don't wave at that Republican," she says.

A part of me wants to say that none of this matters—that politics don't matter, that one person in the White House or the Congress or the Governor's Mansion, doesn't make a speck of difference since he or she occupies only one place in a larger political machinery that, despite its best intentions, ends up doing the world more harm than good.

Still, certain things persist, independent of our politics. In present-day Peru, for example, the place of the tomato's origin, eight species still grow wild in the Andes Mountains. Over centuries people have saved seeds from these tomatoes, domesticated them, transported them across the globe. Today I can grow the same tomato, the Brandywine, an Amish heirloom from 1885, as people did well over one hundred years ago and from all parts of the world—the Galinas from Siberia, the Marmande from France, the Plum Lemon from Moscow, the Principe Borghese from Italy, the Thai Pink Egg, Aunt Ruby's German Green.

But even the tomato at one time couldn't escape being touched by politics. In 1883 Congress passed a tariff act that levied a 10 percent tax on imported vegetables. A few years later a tomato importer challenged the law on the claim that the tomato was a fruit instead of a vegetable and should therefore be free from taxation. The Supreme Court heard the case in 1893 and considered the distinction between *vegetable* and *fruit*. The plaintiff's counsel, after reading definitions of the two words from *Webster's Dictionary*, *Worcester's Dictionary*, and the *Imperial Dictionary*, called two witnesses who had long been fruit and vegetable sellers. One of the witnesses said it was his understanding that the term *fruit* referred to "plants or parts of plants as contain the seeds." The other witness said, "I don't think the term 'fruit' or the term 'vegetables' had, in March, 1883, and prior thereto, any special meaning in trade and commerce in this country different from that which I have read here from the dictionaries." The plaintiff's counsel then read the definition of the word *tomato*. The defense countered by reading the definitions of the words *pea, eggplant, cucumber, squash,* and *pepper*. The plaintiff then read the definitions of *potato, turnip, parsnip, cauliflower, cabbage, carrot,* and *bean*. Neither party presented any other evidence.

In offering the court's ruling, Justice Gray wrote:

> Botanically speaking, tomatoes are fruits of a vine, just as are cucumbers, squashes, beans, and peas. But in the common language of the people . . . all these are vegetables, which are grown in kitchen gardens, and which, whether eaten cooked or raw, are, like potatoes, carrots, parsnips, turnips, beets, cauliflower, cabbage, celery and lettuce, usually served at dinner in, with or after the soup, fish or meats which constitute the principal part of the repast, and not, like fruits generally, as dessert.

The botanical truth that the tomato is indeed a fruit, actually a large berry, held no weight with the court. All the while those eight species of the tomato continued to grow in the Andes, flowering and setting fruit.

My father taught me to keep faith in the seasons, to know that winter gave way to spring, that the earth warmed and seeds germinated and plants grew. So it is year after year. I turn my garden over, work the soil to tilth, plant lettuce and radish seed, cucumbers and pole beans. I set out the tomato seedlings Deb starts in our greenhouse. The bare plot, as summer lengthens, becomes lush with the tall tomato plants, the tepees of pole beans twining up their stakes, the cages of cucumbers. Then the killing frost comes, and then winter's snow and ice, and we wait again for spring and the thawed earth and the chance once more to put our trust in the sunlight and the rain and the plants that grow. How small we are—how insignificant in the light of all this.

I choose to live here in the Midwest, in part because of the way I feel connected to the land and the climate. The flat plains suit me. I listen to friends from the East or West Coast talk about how boring it is to drive across all those *I* states—Indiana, Illinois, and Iowa; to them Ohio is no less mind-numbing and banal—but to me there's something about the way the roads run straight and the farmland stretches out on all sides, plain and unassuming, that comforts me. Perhaps it's my Libra scales that always want to be in balance, but, when I see the predictable landscape that some find lackluster, I feel at home, familiar with the right angles and squared corners. At the same time, I chafe against the fact that, like the landscape, the people here often hold fast to their conservative ways, feel threatened by anything that seems "liberal." They can fence themselves in, close their minds and hearts to the ever-expanding awareness of human rights that is often more accepted in other, more diverse parts of the country. No doubt there's a homogeneity here that numbs, that makes people like my good neighbor Ed believe he has a right to decide what threatens morality.

Sometimes our climate becomes dramatic, and, when it does, it flattens the ego, and maybe that's not a bad thing. Tornadoes, blizzards, droughts. When they come, we huddle in our basements, stay off our streets, ration our water. We feel small in the face of the planet's drama. It reminds us that we don't always stand at its center.

Still, we debate and legislate, sign or don't sign petitions, express our political allegiance or remain silent. We pass Issue 1, in November 2004, and also elect George W. Bush to a second term, a fact that soon stuns the Democrats, who thought John Kerry had the election in the bag because he had a 356,000-vote advantage in Ohio's six largest cities. It's the rural counties and townships that make the difference for Bush. All those good country people I count as my kin turn out in droves to uphold what they consider the sanctity of marriage, and overwhelming numbers of them vote Republican.

So Ed wins, or at least he thinks he does. I really can't talk to him about it now because shortly after the election his company, victims of an economy gone sour, downsizes and he loses his job. Then he sells his house, no longer able to pay the mortgage, and he and Cindy move into an apartment, and I don't see them again. I don't feel happy about this. In all honesty I don't feel any way at all about it.

What I think is this, and I imagine I'll still be thinking it this coming winter when I'm left to shovel my own sidewalk, Ed no longer around to do me the favor: We can participate in a democratic society and think we're making the right choices. We can give leeway to one group while denying the rights of another. We can turn a blind eye to the fact that we're powerless when it comes to the earth turning over, summer's growing season giving way to winter's snows, one year becoming the next until so many have gone by we're stunned by the fact that we stand in the here and now, when it seems like only yesterday we couldn't see it coming to save our lives.

The Classified Ad

The Sumner Press, the weekly paper from my hometown in southeastern Illinois, continues to arrive by mail, even though I've never subscribed to it. A few years ago, when my wife and I were the grand marshals for the town's fall festival parade, the publisher gave us a complimentary one-year subscription. When the subscription ran out, I didn't renew it, but the paper keeps coming as if a higher power has decided I need it in my life. "I don't know why you want that rag in our house," my wife says. She resists its conservative opinions. I'm more inclined to tolerate them, though I don't concur. I've never been able to explain this fully to her, but the truth is I'm happy for the *Press* and the way it allows me to be a voyeur to the comings and goings in this town—population one thousand—in the middle of farmland. Today I take note of the fact that Christmas decorations will soon be up along the main thoroughfare. I see that the Masonic Fish Fry is taking place on this very evening. The Christmas Parade will be on Saturday, December 13. The Community News, which keeps me up on the comings and goings of various citizens, is full, as usual, of items about a certain I.F. and her niece, D.A., who took her aunt to get her hair set and then on to Vincennes, where they did some shopping and enjoyed lunch at the Dogwood Barbecue. M.B. has also done some traveling with her daughter, L.P., and L.P.'s uncle, A.S. The uncle got too tired while the ladies were shopping at Walmart and had to sit on the bench at the front of the store. The correspondent reports that Uncle "doesn't think shopping is any fun." None of this has anything much at all to do with me, outside the fact that I once lived in this place, and that's what I like about it all, the feeling that I can safely eavesdrop on the stories of this town with nothing at risk for myself.

Then I turn to the classified ads, which I never read, but for some reason today I scan them, and what catches my eye is an ad taken out by Judy Beyers of Fort Branch, Indiana. She's looking for her brother, who was born Alvin David Smith to Davis "Smitty" Smith and Velma (Cleeves) Smith in Fort Branch in 1955. Alvin David was, according to the ad, adopted by a couple believed to have lived in Sumner, Illinois. Anyone with information should please contact Judy Beyers by e-mail (address provided) or by phone at the following number. Suddenly I'm no longer a voyeur. I'm the man who has the information that Judy Beyers needs.

But I hesitate, not sure whether I should get involved for fear that I'll encroach on another's right to privacy. Above the Information Wanted ad two columns carry the circuit court clerk's notice of the petition for the acquisition of mineral rights on land owned in Lukin Township. Such rights have been "severed" from the previous owners, which means their period of claim to any discovery of minerals (almost always oil in this county) has run out. In the eyes of the law one's attachment to the land doesn't last forever. It's the word *Lukin* that catches my eye and momentarily takes me away from what I can tell Judy Beyers if I choose.

When I was a boy, I lived on a farm in that township, and I went to a two-room school. I rode on a yellow bus I was supposed to meet on the County Line Road at the end of our lane. For whatever reason my father arranged it so the bus would come all the way down our lane. I wonder now what grounds he had for this special request. Why was I the only kid on the route to get that favor? My mother was a grade school teacher, and surely she'd known her share of parents who lobbied for exceptions on this and that for their sons and daughters. Surely she'd grown weary with their expectations. My father was stern and demanding. He took pride in doing nearly everything he'd been able to do before his accident, and I never knew him to expect anyone to give him an advantage. He farmed his ground, punished his body with the labor, cussed his machinery when it broke down, repaired it when he could, and paid someone else to do the job when the fix was beyond his expertise. He birthed calves, cut hogs, hefted hay bales. Whenever I whined that I couldn't do something, he said, "Can't never did nothing." Why in the world would such a man expect that bus driver to come down our lane?

Could it be because I was an only child, born to older parents, and therefore without older brothers or sisters to accompany me on that walk, to watch over me during the wait for the bus? My mother couldn't provide the escort—she'd be on the way to her own school—and perhaps my father didn't want the chore, busy as he was with this and that on the farm. Or maybe I was too timid, uneasy with new situations. Maybe I balked, and my parents decided to ask for special dispensation. Other children on the route had to walk to the ends of lanes to stand and wait for the bus. I really don't know why my parents thought I shouldn't do likewise, but for some reason they chose to broker a deal. I can only assume that they saw a need, and they decided to do whatever was necessary for my sake. I've never known the desire to protect a son or daughter because my wife and I have no children. She made that decision. I've never had a child then, as my parents did in 1961, to love and keep safe, to put above my own needs and wishes. Perhaps I was more fragile at that time than I remember. I don't even appear in the class photo from my first-grade year because I must have been absent. That was the year I missed fourteen days—clearly the day of the school photo was one of them—because I was "sick." Really, I was homesick, afraid to be away from my house and filled with anxiety. Why? I can speculate that my father's accident and the aftermath jostled my world so much that I clung to habit, desperate for stability and comfort. Change brought back what my father's accident surely imprinted on me—the unsettling feeling that I could be swept away or that when I wasn't watchful something could happen to change my home forever. When my father was in the hospital, I was whisked off to my aunt's. After he came home he was, as she would tell me later, a shattered man full of frayed nerves and temper. He filled our home with his anger, and I was left forever with the feeling that I could never trust what I thought was mine. In an instant everything could change.

So Judy Beyers is somewhere right now, not knowing a thing about me, and here I sit, reading about the Lawrence County Housing Authority and how it's accepting applications for low-rent housing. I even take time to research the county's demographics, letting an Internet search excuse me from deciding whether to tell Judy what I know. Close to sixteen thousand people live in the county, located across the Wabash River from Vincennes, Indiana, and 13.1 percent of those people live below the poverty line in a county that has always been mostly agricultural. Even in 1961, when I started first grade, most of the farmers were barely getting by. My parents were fairly flush because of my mother's teaching position, a job she would lose the summer between my first and second-grade years because the school board thought she had too many problems disciplining her students. I remember plenty of families, though—larger families than my own—who were tapped out and providing for their kids as best they could. When I look at the school photos from that time, I can see, despite the scrubbed faces and bright smiles, all the signs of stretched budgets: the haircuts done at home, the beat-up shoes, the clothes handed down from older brothers and sisters, or in some cases the same outfits, when they still fit, worn year to year for the photo because those clothes were the best some of us had. So we were farm kids going to a two-room school that sat off the Sumner-Lancaster blacktop just a little ways down a gravel road from the Bethlehem church. A two-room school in the middle of all that farmland. A bus to tote us down dirt and gravel roads, past farmhouses and barns and livestock pens, over creeks that rose above their banks in spring, beneath high skies lined with contrails from jets or leaden with clouds. In winter we breathed on the glass of the bus windows and wrote our names with our gloved fingers, as if to leave evidence, which of course would vanish, that once upon a time we were there: Dale and Cynda Thacker; Larry and Dan Brian; Tony Hair; Alan Correll; Rick Lewis; Becky Hasewinkle; Tammy Marks; Stella and Della Jackson; their sisters Alberta and Rose; Esther and Steve Jackman; The Yows, Alice and Eugene and Fred; the Wrights, Alma and Mary and their cousin Laedus; Lloyd Linder; Linda Brines; Jim Harness; Bobbi Riggs; David Sidebottom. When I look at the school photo now, I can name all twenty-seven of us, grades one through eight, at this itty-bitty school in this itty-bitty township, where every morning or afternoon, we climbed on or off the bus, farm kids whose lives were linked by the fact that we lived along those township roads. Back then it felt like our entire lives were meant to be lived between the boundaries of those roads that ran at straight angles. We'd always been there, and we always would. We'd know one another forever.

From the classified ad rates listed in the *Press*, I see that the first twenty words of Judy Beyers's ad cost her four dollars. Each additional word, forty-three of them, cost her twenty cents apiece. Twelve dollars and sixty cents total, a reasonable sum to spend on a shot at finding a brother.

"I think I know him," I say to my wife. "The man she's looking for. I think I went to school with him."

"Are you sure?"

"Not entirely. But I remember this kid."

I more than remember him. David Sidebottom—for some reason I remember that, even though we called him David, his first name was Alvin—lived on the Gilead Church Road. Like me, he was the son of older parents. They lived in a run-down house on my bus route. In my memory I can see him running out of that house and bounding up onto the bus, swiping at his drippy nose with his coat sleeve in the winter, carrying with him the smell of hot cooking grease. His parents didn't have, as my father used to say, "as much as a pot to piss in." A question I keep mulling over is how in 1955—if indeed I have the right family—a couple like that, poor and aged, would have managed to adopt a baby. Would it have been an adoption that was on the square, or would it have been a deal brokered for whatever reason because the birth parents couldn't care for the child and there happened to be this kindly old couple willing to take him on?

My wife says, "I wonder if he knows that he was adopted."

I've been wondering that too. "He might not even know he has a sister."

"So what are you going to do?"

"I might be the only one who can help her."

I e-mail Judy Beyers to say I may have information that will help her find her brother, but the e-mail bounces back. I double check the address and try sending the message again.

Back it comes. Here it sits in my in-box, this message that says, here are the facts you may need to know. For some reason cyberspace is no respecter of this possible sibling reunion, and that breaks my heart because I'm thinking about this man and the sister who is looking for him and the information I hold that can't make its way to the person who needs it.

Sister. The word has always sounded sweet to me. I've always longed for one of my own. When I was young, I often convinced myself that I was living a story, the beginning of which I didn't even know. How else could I explain what seemed to me extraordinary—my parents who were so much older than the parents of my friends, my father with those hooks and the rage he brought into our home after his accident. In the story I conjured, I found refuge with an older sister, one I didn't know I had—we'd been separated for some reason, and I'd been taken in by this timid woman and this angry man. My sister in my story somehow found me and took me away from my father's rage. His hooks could grasp his belt, a yardstick, a switch cut from a persimmon tree, and he could whip me about my legs and buttocks until welts appeared, and I sobbed with a raw ache because, when the whip-

pings came and for a good while after they were done, I believed
that my father didn't love me. Even if he could convince a school
board to allow a bus to drive all the way down our lane, it didn't
mean he cared for me at all. A sister to protect me. I felt my mother's love, her tenderness, but she was too timid to stand up in the
face of my father's anger. I've never blamed her for that. I've always thought of her as a kind woman who loved me the best she
could—perhaps loved me more because she knew she was powerless and the only thing she could give me was love and a sense
of what it was to endure.

When the e-mail to Judy Beyers keeps bouncing back, I consider for a moment, as I'm prone to do, that this is the universe's
way of telling me something—telling me, perhaps, that this is
none of my business. Maybe Alvin David Sidebottom, if he truly
is Alvin David Smith, doesn't want to be found. Maybe cyberspace is telling me to leave well enough alone.

But I can't. I think of all the times I've posted queries on geneal-
ogy Web boards and relied on the kindness of strangers to provide
information about ancestors. The Martins and Reads (my mother's side of the family) left little in the way of written documents,
left few footprints as they passed through the world, and, when I
went searching for what I could find, it was often people who had
no stake in the matter at all who gave me what I needed to know.

So I call the number in Judy Beyers's ad, and I get her voice mail.
I leave a message that says, "This may not be anything at all, but
I thought you should have the information in case it helps you."

I go on to tell her I was born in 1955, the same year as her brother,
and I went to school in the country about ten miles from Sumner with a boy named Alvin David. I remember that his parents
were an older couple. I remember they didn't have much. I leave
my phone number in case she wants to talk.

I hang up and think, Well, there, at least I've done what I can. Maybe I've given her nothing that'll matter at all. Let whatever forces that guide us through the world take it from here.

My mother always told me, nights when I couldn't fall asleep, "Just count your blessings, and they'll give you peace."

I often had trouble sleeping when I was young. I was a sleep-walker, a sleep talker, a boy who had all sorts of nightmares, a boy who slept on a sofa bed in the living room and sometimes woke in the night to the headlights of cars that crept halfway down the lane, trying to see if anyone was home. People bent on thievery. My father sometimes threatened to give me to the Gypsies. I thought anything was possible.

Judy Beyers calls back. She calls a few minutes after I leave my voice mail, and she tells me she's talked with her cousin, who is older and who remembers more about Alvin David. Yes, he was adopted by an older couple. Yes, they were poor. "What did he look like?" she asks me. "This boy?"

I can hear the excitement in her voice, the trembling. She's closer to finding her brother than she's ever been.

"A small boy," I said, "with dark hair."

"Dark complexion?"

"Yes."

"Oh, Lord. I'm shaking. You're the first person who's tried to help me. What do I do now?"

How overwhelmed Judy seems, nearly paralyzed with the thought that she might be close to finding her brother, so much so that she can't figure out her next move. I give her some suggestions. I tell her I've read about a Pam Sidebottom in the *Sumner Press*. She serves on the Bridgeport City Council. Bridgeport is the small town five miles east of Sumner on Route 250. It's another three miles east along that highway to Lawrenceville, the county seat.

"Could be his wife?" I say to Judy with a question in my voice to let her know I'm willing to speculate with her. "Maybe he's still in the area?"

I suggest that she go to the County Clerk's office in the Lawrenceville courthouse—her home in Fort Branch is only about forty miles away—and see if she can find property tax records or the like that will locate an address for Alvin David Sidebottom. Once I'm off the phone and giving the matter more thought, I decide to see what I can find out via the Internet. It doesn't take me long to do a people search and to find an entry for an Alvin D. Sidebottom, age fifty-two, living in Lawrenceville, Illinois. I e-mail Judy—she told me the *Press* left a dot out of her address, so now I know to add it, and cyberspace, appeased, is finally sympathetic to the efforts to locate lost siblings—and tell her what I've found. "I'm going to see if I can find an address or a phone number," I write, but I'm not willing to pay the cost required to get further records through PeopleFinders or Intelius—the cost is minimal, but I always balk at using a credit card online for fear of identity theft. I recognize the irony of my desire to protect my own identity while at the same time I'm doing all I can to reveal someone else's. Again, I consider the fact that Alvin David Sidebottom may not want to be found. I wonder whether I'm doing the right thing.

My wife, by nature a very private person, says, "You better hope this has a good end."

I do. I hope that with all my heart, but at the same time I'm a little nervous. I wonder how much Alvin David remembers about me and the moment at the Lukin School that had such a profound effect on me, one of those moments that happens in a kid's life and then stays with him all the years ahead. So much of what I've written, both in fiction and nonfiction, comes, however indirectly, from that time in school when our teacher, Mrs. Watts, decided we'd operate under the Old Testament law of an eye for an eye. Whatever we did to someone else would be returned to us. It sounds barbaric from our perspective now, but I suppose it was meant as a lesson to us that our actions had serious consequences, that no one gets away clean, that, when we touch the world, the world touches back.

One day Alvin David kicked me in the leg, and my teacher brought us to the front of the room and demanded that I kick him back. Why had he kicked me? I can only speculate. Maybe it was just kids roughhousing, or maybe somewhere deep down he resented me because I was good at my lessons and he wasn't or because my family was more comfortable than his when it came to money. Maybe that fact canceled out what we shared—children, as we were, of older parents. For whatever reason he kicked me, and I was in the uncomfortable position of having to return that kick. I didn't want to. I was too shy. I also knew the lash of my father's belt and how it made me ache inside. The truth was I felt sorry for Alvin David, who had so little, and I didn't want to hurt him. So I gave him a tap on the shin. I wanted to obey my teacher. I wanted to do what my friends expected. In truth, however, I would have preferred to go back to my desk and pretend that nothing had happened. Inside, though I had no way of articulating this then, the compassion I'd learned from my mother was at war with the brutality I'd taken in from my father. I'd live years and years from that point trying to reconcile those two opposing parts of myself. I still do somewhat, but I imagine people would find that hard to believe since the even-keeled part of me is more prevalent. Temper, though, is never too far below the surface. That day in the schoolroom I tried to do Alvin David a favor. I tapped him. I looked him in the eye, hoping he'd understand. All he did, though, was laugh, leaving me to feel humiliated and angry, beat upon and small—leaving me years and years to work out the place empathy has in the midst of an unkind world.

So my wife says I should hope I'm not meddling in family business that's not my concern. "It could be a delicate situation," she says.

Her parents adopted her brother when she was ten years old, and, as an adult, when he set out to find his birth parents, she told him what little she knew and encouraged his efforts. Why, then, do I sense that she's resisting this story of someone else's discovery? Why do I feel that she'd rather I not be a part of it?

"I'm just telling her what I know," I say.

And that's when I think about the picture.

"I have a school photo that has Alvin David in it," I write to Judy. "I could scan it and e-mail it to you if you think that might be helpful."

I'm fully invested in this now, perhaps because I sense something unresolved in my history with Alvin David. It's the unsettled feeling of contradictory impulses at work that rose up in me that day when I was expected to return his kick that has fueled so much of what I've put between the margins of pages over the years. In some ways I owe a career to him. If he hadn't laughed at me that day at school, maybe I wouldn't have learned the significance of choice and consequence as powerfully as I did. Maybe I wouldn't have to try to work out the simultaneous pull between empathy and temper in nearly everything I write. Still, there's a part of me that pays attention to my wife's reluctance. Somehow I'm afraid to be involved in this story of Alvin David, this story I'm helping along. Maybe I'm afraid that my wife is right. Maybe the story she's spinning in her head, as she imagines the outcome, comes from a lack of faith in the ties that bind. Her own family history is one of dissent and severance—family members who stop speaking to each other, petty arguments that explode into full-blown feuds. She's not even very close to her brother now. They go months and months without speaking because of a falling out precipitated by my sister-in-law. Maybe my wife suspects that Alvin David won't welcome his sister into his life and he'll blame me for my part in the reunion. Could it be that my wife even hopes for that outcome as evidence of the impossibility of family, thereby convincing herself that her own family story is more often the norm?

"OMG," Judy says in her e-mail response. Although I'm not one who sends text messages, I know that the abbreviation is for "Oh My God" and is meant to convey excitement. "That would be absolutely wonderful!"

I scan the photo and send it to her, identifying Alvin David as the boy in the front row, third from the left. A little boy with scuffed, ankle-high brogans and what I'm sure were the best clothes he had, a pair of what we called wash pants back then, heavy cotton Chino trousers, the legs too short so his bare shins show above his socks, and a white polo shirt, a crest on the pocket and a dark stain around the crest.

Judy replies: "omg. i am almost positive it is him, i am taking my laptop up to my cousins right now, she will know for absolute certain." She doesn't take the time to capitalize or worry about punctuation. That's how excited she is and in a hurry to share the photo with her cousin. She closes with what I hope remains a blessing even once this story is resolved: "you are an angel lee."

Just above Judy's classified ad is a Card of Thanks notice that expresses appreciation for kindnesses shown during a family member's illness and death. One family says good-bye to a loved one taken too soon, while a sister sets out to find her brother.

"Linda looked at the picture as did other family members," Judy writes to me. "We compared it to pictures of young boys in the family and there is such a likeness, if it is not him then it should be, lol." The first time someone used *lol* in an e-mail to me, I had no idea what it meant. If I had my own kids, I more than likely would have known it was text lingo for "laughing out loud." "I have a picture of my dad when he was a young man and even tho I have never seen either of them in person, I am certain it is him."

Alvin David, she means. Her brother. She tells me that she called the sheriff's department in Lawrenceville, and, though the dispatcher couldn't legally tell her anything, she gave Judy reason to believe that she had the right city. The dispatcher suggested that she come to the water department or the post office to see if she could get an address.

"I'm going to Lawrenceville on Saturday," she writes. "I'm going to see what I can find out."

I don't hear anything from her that day or evening or on Sunday, and though I'm curious, I resist the inclination to e-mail her and ask for information. I worry that Judy didn't find him. I worry that she found him and things didn't go well. I tell myself that in the long run it's none of my business. Then on Sunday evening I call my voice mail at the university to listen to messages, and I hear a man's voice. "Mr. Martin," he says, "this is Mr. Sidebottom. Alvin David Sidebottom." The voice has that unmistakable southern Illinois twang, a flavor from the Kentucky of so many of our ancestors. A curt voice set about its business. A voice I haven't heard in forty-six years, a little husky now with age or nerves. The voice of a man with something on his mind. "I'll be back in touch with you," he says. "You can count on that."

That's it. That's all he has to say, and I'm left with the unsettling feeling that he's called out of anger. The repetition of *Mr.* Did he use that with sarcasm? As in "*Mr.* Martin, this is *Mr.* Sidebottom. As in, "Who in the hell do you think you are? What right do you have in my business?"

I tell my wife about the voice mail. She lifts her eyebrows as if to say, "See what I told you?"

Then another e-mail comes from Judy, but it does nothing to make me feel better. All it says is, "I found him, and, yes, it *was* him."

I respond. "I hope the reunion was something he welcomed."

She doesn't answer, which worries me even more. I'm afraid there's been an ugly scene and she can't bring herself to tell me about it.

I rarely answer the phone when it rings at our house, preferring to leave that to my wife, but tonight I'm standing right by it, and she says, "You get it."

"Is this Lee Martin?" the man on the other end of the line asks, and I tell him it is. "This is Alvin Sidebottom," he says. "I finally got your home number from my sister." He clears his throat, and his voice gets softer. "I'm calling to say thank you."

I carry the cordless phone upstairs, leaving my wife downstairs, so I can have privacy. We're in the holiday season, and, as I talk to Alvin David from my study, I look out the window at my neighbor's light display across the street: white icicle lights from the gutters, outlines of sleighs and snowmen on the lawn, multicolored lights in the shrubs, sparkling miniature Christmas trees along the driveway, carols playing over a speaker. The whole shebang is on a timer, and at regular intervals the lights go out for a few moments and then flash back on. I've always thought it an overly elaborate display, and I've taken to referring to the neigh-

bor as Clark Griswold after the Christmasphile played by Chevy
Chase in *Christmas Vacation*. "Is your house on fire, Clark?" his
aunt asks him in one scene. "No, Aunt Bethany," he answers,
"those are the Christmas lights."

Last year the neighbor had the lights up before Halloween. This
year he waited until November 1 to start the show. I'm a man who
likes to keep his holidays separate. Something about jumping the
gun seems like force-feeding to me, spooning out the Christmas
cheer before the calendar says it's time. It's not that I'm a Scrooge.
It's just that I believe there's a proper time, and, if someone like
my Clark Griswold wannabe neighbor lights up before that time,
well, that's just smug. That's saying he's got a better life than the
rest of us "unadorned" folks, and, by god, he's got the lights and
the music to prove it.

Tonight, though, I'm grateful for those lights because they
make a perfect backdrop for the story Alvin David tells me about
Judy and her cousin showing up at his door. The cousin stood a
bit forward on the step, Judy slightly behind her.

"Was your dad Joe Smith?" the cousin asked.

"That's right," said Alvin David.

So he knew he was adopted.

"And your mother was Velma Cleeves?"

"Right again."

The cousin stepped back and pulled Judy around to her side.
"Meet your sister," the cousin said, and, well, as Alvin David says
to me on the phone, "I just about fell over."

Later I learn from Judy that she and Alvin David had the same
father but different mothers. Judy was adopted too, and when
she was eighteen she found her father's family. By that time he
was dead. She knew about Alvin David, knew she had this half-
brother, and for years she'd tried to find him.

"The funny thing is," he tells me, "I used to drive a truck, and I made deliveries just a couple of blocks from her house in Fort Branch."

That's where he is now. I can hear the noise of conversation and laughter in the background, the sounds of a holiday gathering. He's at his sister's house with the family he never knew, and I'm looking at my neighbor's lights, an ache rising in my throat because my parents are long gone, because I'm an only child, because I have no children of my own, because this year at Christmas it'll be, as it always is, my wife and I alone in our house.

I'm listening to Alvin David as he tells me how he's sitting there right now with his sister and his cousins, and I can hear the wonder in his voice, like how in the heck did this happen. I'm thinking about that time at the Lukin School when he kicked me and I had to kick him back and he laughed at me. I want to ask him if he remembers that, but then he says, "When Judy told me someone I went to Lukin with called her, I knew it had to be you."

"Why would you think that?" I'm genuinely puzzled. All these years I've remembered that kick, remembered his face breaking into laughter, remembered that humiliation. "I moved away before third grade. I wouldn't even think you'd remember me."

"Oh, I remember you," he says. "You were about the only friend I had back then."

He catches me off guard, and I don't know what to say. When I look at that school photo, I can pick out the boys who were my closest friends, and he isn't on the list. I even recall participating in one or two tricks played on him. He fills the silence now by giving me his address. I write it down. He wants to stay in touch, he says. He's going to send me a picture of him as soon as he can have one made so I can see what he looks like now. He's enthusiastically friendly, and I can't bring myself to mention the time he kicked me. Besides, his line about me being his only friend is enough, if I let it be, to tell me he does remember that kick and, what's more, he understands now in a way he didn't then that, when I tapped him, I was doing him a kindness. He pauses to say to someone there with him, "Sure, I'll take another one," and I assume he's talking about something to eat or drink, and I suddenly feel as if I'm keeping him from his party.

"It's some story, isn't it?" I say to him.

"Yes, sir. It is indeed."

He thanks me again, and we say good-bye. My neighbor's lights have gone off, and I wait for them to come on again, but it's late, and the timer has shut them down for the rest of the night, and I stand there, holding to myself what's just happened with Alvin David, keeping it a secret just a bit longer before telling it to my wife.

"Who was it?" she asks, when I go downstairs.

"Alvin David Sidebottom."

She nods. "Somehow I knew it was him."

I tell her the whole story, including the part about him saying I was his only friend. "It's a happy ending," I say.

We're turning off lights, getting ready to go to bed. I think of how I came to my parents unexpectedly in the middle of their lives, how Glen and Reba Sidebottom adopted a little boy so they wouldn't be alone.

"I'm glad," my wife says, and she seems genuinely happy about the way things have turned out for Alvin David and Judy. I've been wrong to imagine that she wished otherwise, and that makes me feel guilty for everything I've learned to keep to myself. I don't tell her that I often wonder what our child would have been like had we ever had one. I don't say that in the secret, most inner part of me I mourn the fact that she always refused to have children. I don't tell her that in some ways this story of Alvin David

Sidebottom has left me feeling as content as I've been in some time, nor do I tell her that a part of me thinks of him tonight with his new family—I remember the sounds of laughter filling his sister's house—and I long for everything he now has. I turn off the last light, and there's a moment so still before my wife and I move toward the stairs, move through the dark, through the quiet, here at the end of our day.

A Backward Spring

It's mid-September in Texas, and I'm stripping the dead leaves from our Caddo maple. I close my hand around the whippet branches and pull toward the tips; dry, coppery leaves crumble and fall to the ground. I keep their dust on my skin.

The Caddo maple, according to our local horticulturalist, is an ideal, much-underused tree for North Texas, but ours, planted in February, has yet to take hold. In spring the buds swelled, and green leaves opened but never matured. They drooped from the branches, tiny and wrinkled, like babies' hands. Now the nursery owner has nicked a branch with a pocketknife and shown me the green heartwood. "There's plenty of moisture in it," he's said. He's told me to strip away the dead leaves so the tree won't concentrate its energy on feeding them. "Water it a couple of times a week," he's said. "If it's going to make it, we'll know soon."

My wife, Deb, tells this story to her mother the next time they talk on the phone, even though she knows her mother won't be able to recall it. My mother-in-law is losing threads of memory.

People, places, episodes—all of them slip away from her as soon as they occur. She no longer has the ability to retrieve them. She's sixty-four, and her neurologist suspects the onset of Alzheimer's, a suspicion that so far we've kept secret from her. Already naturally prone to depression, she's the sort that worries something to death. We're afraid that, if we told her about the illness, her condition would deteriorate more quickly than it will if she doesn't know about it. "Do you know the date?" the neurologist asked her at their first meeting. "The day of the week? The president of the United States?"

"Al Gore," she said.

The neurologist chuckled. "You're a very smart lady, Mrs. Goss. You may know something we don't."

The first time Deb took me home to meet her mother, it was eleven o'clock at night, and, after an exchange of strained pleasantries, my future mother-in-law excused herself, went down the hallway to her bedroom, and locked the door. It would be years before she would finally decide that I was a decent sort and not the bogeyman she had feared that first evening.

Now her illness has accentuated her natural inclination toward paranoia. She draws the drapes around the corners of the rods and pins them to the wall; she makes sure the panels overlap in the middle, which she also pins together. She wants no gaps, no slivers of space where someone might be able to see into her house. She refuses to pick up the phone until she hears a familiar voice on the answering machine. If she's alone in her house, all the windows and doors locked, and she wants to tell someone something private, she'll come close and whisper, afraid someone might be lurking outside, trying to eavesdrop.

Deb tells me that she always remembers her mother being afraid, and there are hints of this in a few letters my mother-in-law wrote to Deb's father when he was in the army. My mother-in-law would have been nineteen at the time, working in town at the Weber Medical Clinic and living with her parents out in the country. "The folks are going to town for a little while," she says in one letter, "and I don't want to stay home by myself, but I haven't told them yet." In another letter she talks about coming home from work one evening when she knew her parents had gone to visit friends. "I got the car in the garage," she says, "and locked the doors." Like now, she didn't want anyone to know she was there.

Since my father-in-law's death six years ago, she's been lonely and eager for company. She has a few friends with whom she goes shopping or out to dinner or to singles' dances, but most evenings she's in her house, crocheting, the television on for the noise. Some nights, late, she calls us in Texas and talks about how depressed she is. Other widows snap up boyfriends at the singles' dances, she says, but not her. "I don't know what's wrong with me," she says.

In all honesty, even before her problems with memory, she's always been a difficult woman to tolerate. She's often too forward, quick to comment on other peoples' flaws. If she's in a public place and she sees someone she considers too thin, too fat, too overdressed, too—you fill in the blank—she makes no effort to hide her disapproval. "Look at that," she'll say in a too-loud voice. "What a sight." Privacy, which she values so much for herself, doesn't seem to be a concern when she speaks of others. Even her own family isn't safe. She once told a near stranger that her brother-in-law's testicles had swollen to the size of grapefruits. Another time, on an Amtrak train, she announced that Deb was in the lavatory "washing her privates."

Still, there are times when my mother-in-law is sweet and play-ful and generous. She gets a kick out of a good joke; she loves to make Christmas candies and give them to people. She often goes out of her way to be friendly to her neighbors, to help other widows with their shopping, to prepare hot dishes for church suppers. Still, if we weren't family, it's doubtful that we'd be friends. She's obsessively neat, bundling garbage in layers of paper towel, plastic wrap, paper bags, before tossing it in the trash can. She's judgmental, quick to condemn people who differ from her own sense of moral behavior. She gossips about the divorcée who lives across the street, pointing out over and over that a certain gentleman's car was in front of the house until three o'clock in the morning. "Isn't that terrible?" she says, anxious for someone to agree.

I have to admit that over the years I've often been glad to live at some distance from her and her outrageous behavior while at the same time knowing that in some ways we're alike—both of us anxious for order, both of us afraid of being alone. I don't know exactly when she decided that I was a decent sort, someone to love and trust, but I'm determined now to be kind to her, to be tolerant and understanding and helpful. My own mother suffered from senile dementia as a result of a series of small strokes, and I know the frustrations and sorrows of watching someone you love disappear.

It's been seventeen years since Deb and I lived close to our families, and it'll be a few years more before we move to Columbus, Ohio, a five-hour drive from "home" in Illinois. We've lived in Arkansas, Ohio once before, Tennessee, Nebraska, Virginia, and now in Texas, as we've pursued graduate degrees and teaching positions. Last spring, when the opportunity to return to the Midwest presented itself, a chance to be a mere three-hour-drive from my mother-in-law, it seemed at first so simple to say yes. But forces of time and circumstance conspired to make the decision a difficult one. We had just begun to notice my mother-in-law's memory lapses and hadn't wanted to consider that they might be a sign of Alzheimer's. Therefore, the fact that she might be ill didn't occur to us and didn't enter into our decision-making process, as it surely would have had we known. Deb and I, in the end, decided to stay in Texas. We had become disgusted with moving. We had had our fill of boxes and packing tape and change of address cards and trusting our possessions to moving companies.

For those of us who have long wished for a permanent home, a place can tie us to it in short order. We can invest so much in the effort that we find it difficult to leave. When we finally settled in Texas, Deb and I gave thanks. We bought a house that had been somewhat neglected and set out to revive it. We landscaped and nurtured the lawn, put up rain gutters, and painted. This is it, we thought. This is home. This is where we stay.

Once at a rest stop along Interstate 55 in Arkansas, a man asked me how to get to Illinois. It was the day before Thanksgiving, late afternoon, and Deb and I were on our way from Memphis, where we lived at the time, to her parents' home in southern Illinois, a part of the state known as "Egypt."

The man's question surprised me. He wasn't just asking how to locate a town, a neighborhood, a street, an address; he wanted to know how to find a state. He was putting down the hood on his car, an old station wagon with Texas plates. How could anyone, I wondered, set out from home on a journey of any length without knowing exactly how to reach his destination? What was I to tell this man? "When you get to Missouri, turn right?" He was wide-eyed and boyish, his face reddened by the cold. He had no coat and stood on the concrete walkway stamping his feet. His shirt cuffs, unbuttoned, flapped around his bony wrists. He needed information, and I was the one he was trusting to give it.

So I stuck to the facts. "Stay on 55," I told him, "until you hit I-57. You'll cross the river at Cairo, and you'll be in Illinois. That's where I'm headed too."

Did I add the last part, the fact of my own destination, because I wished to chide him by pointing out that I knew my route and implying that he should too? Or did I sense a similarity, a shared longing for home, I couldn't have then articulated? Was I telling him we were both in the same boat?

"Do you know Willow Hill?" he asked.

As a matter of fact, I did. It was a small town no more than twenty miles north of where I was going. I had passed through Willow Hill countless times during the six years my parents and I lived in Oak Forest, a suburb of Chicago. We made the five-hour trip back to our farm on weekends and holidays, and Willow Hill was one of the towns I always eagerly awaited since it signaled that our journey was almost at an end. That it should be the town where this man was going amazed me.

"I know it," I told him. "Sure. Willow Hill."

"I got a wife there I ain't seen in thirteen years." He smiled a big old cat-that-ate-the-canary grin. Then he shook his head, and his grin turned a bit sheepish, as if he were thinking, My, oh my, won't she be surprised.

Although ten years have passed since that day, I still wonder what happened that night when he finally got to Willow Hill. Did he find his wife? Did she let him into her house? Or did she shut the door in his face, leave him scratching his head, feeling like a dope, wondering what he could have been thinking to have traveled so far?

In Genesis, when "famine was over all the face of the earth," Jacob sent his sons from their home in the land of Canaan down into Egypt to buy corn. They had no way of knowing that the brother they had sold into slavery, Joseph, was now the governor of the land and that he was the one who had directed the storing

up of grain from seven years of abundant harvest. When he finally revealed himself to his brothers, they were ashamed, but he
told them not to grieve; his presence in Egypt, though it had re-
sulted from their own cruelty, had turned out to be necessary to
their survival. If he hadn't come to Egypt, become governor, and
had the wisdom to store the grain, what would they do now for
food? "So now it was not you that sent me hither," he said, "but
God" (Genesis 45:8).

I spent the first twenty-five years of my life in Illinois, most
of them in "Egypt," where my father owned an eighty-acre farm.
Although I've lived many places since, I've usually managed to
find something to keep me connected to home: snow and ice, apple orchards and strawberry farms, cornfields and forests of oak,
maple, hickory, beech, and sweet gum. But in north Texas weeks
can pass in the summer without rain; temperatures in the mid-
nineties signal a cool spell. The heat lasts deep into October, and
the autumn colors of the trees are drab in comparison with the
brilliant woodlands of the Midwest. A Texas winter is really not a
winter at all. Perhaps one or two days will bring a dusting of snow
that melts away in quick order or an ice storm that slicks things
up for an hour or two. It's not uncommon for the temperatures
to reach the sixties, even the seventies. For a native midwesterner
it seems like cheating to live here during the winter. I watch The
Weather Channel for video of blizzards, and I feel nostalgia and
longing and guilt and relief.

Story has it that southern Illinois became known as "Egypt"
after the harsh winter of 1830–31, during which snow to the depth
of three feet covered the northern part of the state and frost lasted
well into May. It was, as one source puts it, "a very backward
spring." The killing frost came again on September 10, ruining
the unripened corn. The only ears to mature properly were in the

fields of southern Illinois. Folks from the north drove their wagons south to buy corn, claiming that, like the sons of Jacob, they were going down to Egypt.

Whenever I return to that part of the country now, no matter the season, I know immediately the way grass greens in the spring and how the earth smells as it thaws. I know the humid days of summer, the air dusted with corn pollen, the rich scent of autumn, leaves firing red and yellow and orange and then dying away and falling to rot on the ground. I know the snows of winter and the wind screaming across the flat prairie.

I am the one who renounced this land, went away to college—the first Martin to do so—and became a teacher and a writer instead of working the family farm. After my parents were dead, I leased those eighty acres and finally sold them the year I came to Texas. There are times here when I feel my life is blessed. Each spring I plant onions and radishes and lettuce and potatoes. Later I set out tomato plants and cucumber vines. My garden is a raised bed nine feet by twelve feet, a mere sliver when compared to the large gardens my parents used to tend. Still, when I press my hands into the soil—when I water and hoe and harvest—I feel a kinship with all the Martins who were at one time farmers in southern Illinois, in that land of "Egypt" where my mother-in-law, day by day, forgets. Each time we speak on the phone, I feel guilty because Deb and I aren't there.

By October the Caddo maple is still leafless. In our garden our pole beans—Kentucky Wonders—have wrapped their tendrils around the twine supports Deb has draped over a ridge pole and stretched taut to stakes in the ground. She's built the skeleton of a house in our garden—an A-frame formed by two sets of crossing poles, one set at each end of the garden and a long pole laid into the crotches. The twine ribbons down on both sides. Soon this will be a house of green, the palmlike leaves of the Kentucky Wonders bushing out and then setting the long, narrow fingers of beans.

The evening I helped Deb build this frame, I thought of the way my own parents had spent years working side by side in their garden. I remembered the way my father, ordinarily a gruff man, would sometimes come in from hoeing and say to my mother in a soft voice, heavy with sorrow and regret, "I cut down a bean plant. You ought to shoot me. That's how worthless I am."

To me, when I was a teenager, my parents' garden was the place where I had to work when I would rather have been somewhere else. I cursed the rototiller that jarred me, the weeds that grew up and had to be cut down, the hoe handle that left blisters on my palms. But, despite my aversion to this plot of ground and the work that tied me to it, I was learning, through my parents' reverence, a respect for everything that grew and the seasons that dictated the time allowed each living thing.

It pains me, then, to see the Caddo maple, bare branched, here at the beginning of fall, when its leaves should just be starting to yellow and become glorious with color. And, when my mother-in-law phones and tells the same stories barely minutes apart or fails to remember episodes from our visit in the summer, I mourn the fact that neurofibrils are tangling in her brain, pairs of filaments wrapping around each other to form helixes. I grieve for everything that my mother-in-law doesn't know she's forgotten: the tomatoes she bought at the farmers' market; how to balance a checkbook; the needlework of crochet, its weaving of looped stitches from a single thread.

In my garden the tendrils of the Kentucky Wonders snake up the twine supports, and their steady advance—the fresh growth of leaves come from seed—renews my faith in the value of all our days. In the sixteenth- and seventeenth-century English Renaissance, knot gardens were popular—herb gardens planted in an interlocking design to signify infinity. The knot motif had been used in the decorative arts of Rome, Islamic countries, and Medieval Europe. The traditional Islamic garden was meant to be a safe and sacred place, designed to reflect universal unity and order. Imagine the herbs woven together—lavenders and basils, rues and thymes—looping and threading a single line that seems to have no beginning or end.

From my parents I have inherited a penchant for straight rows. My father marked off his with strings stretched between two sticks; he followed that string with the blade of an old-fashioned single-shear cultivator, leaving a shallow furrow for the seeds we would plant. I can still hear the singing click of the cultivator's wheel and the evening birdsong that serenaded us as we worked. I can feel the cool air of early spring, can see the dazzling green of the grass.

I remember all this because acetylcholine in the limbic system of my brain has carried the memory—visual, auditory, and kinesthetic—from short-term memory to long-term storage in my temporal lobe. The image of my parents and I working in the garden is there—the sights, the sounds, the muscular movement—in a vast chain of brain cells that neurologists call "memory traces." Each cell in the chain holds only a small portion of the complete memory.

Alzheimer's patients suffer from a shortage of acetylcholine. Even though a portion of a memory trace may still be intact within a neuron, it may be unable to connect with other bits of the same memory because not enough acetylcholine exists to transport it. Migration, then, is short-circuited by the tangled filaments in the hippocampus. People like my mother-in-law lack the biological ability to send memories to long-term storage and, over time, become unable to retrieve the memory traces that already exist.

One winter evening in Arkansas, where Deb and I, on our way to Illinois, had stopped for the night, I went running in a thick fog. The vapor lights in the parking lots of the motels and restaurants were dim and fuzzy. Suddenly, I heard the honk of geese and raised my head just in time to see the skein passing over, each goose a black silhouette against the gray fog. Although I was delighted by their appearance, I was also swayed by their confident navigation through the fog. I was in a place I didn't know, trying to keep my bearings. Deb was waiting for me in our motel room, already having told me to be careful not to get lost.

My mother-in-law, from time to time, forgets where she lives. Her friends have told stories about being in the car with her on occasions when she stopped in the middle of the street and said, "I can't remember how to get home." Once she and a friend were traveling down a highway talking about the cornfields they were passing, when the car started to veer off the road. My mother-in-law's friend shouted at her, and, after the car was back on course, my mother-in-law said, "I forgot I was driving. My word."

It's unsettling, of course, to hear stories like these, not only because they signal a need for intervention but also because we don't like to think of our loved ones losing a steady foothold on the earth. We like to believe we're all anchored and capable of choosing navigation, that visible proof of our control over space, that movement that allows us, even if it is an illusion, to believe we can conquer time. Why else do we marvel over the migrations of birds, butterflies, sea animals—those instinctual journeys sometimes over thousands of miles, such efforts of faith? A ruby-throated hummingbird, a mere sixth of an ounce in weight, flies from New Hampshire forests to Costa Rica. Painted lady butterflies leave the Sahara Desert and cross the Mediterranean Sea on the power of their dainty wings. Humpback whales swim through oceans following the geomagnetic field of the Earth, even when that field fluctuates and draws them to land. Often, a beached whale, when towed back to the sea, will again swim to shore, convinced that it's moving in the right direction.

At the edge of our neighborhood developers are clearing twenty-three acres of pastureland to make room for houses and apartment buildings. Where once there were mesquite trees and cacti and yucca, where each spring wildflowers bloomed—bluebonnets and Indian paintbrushes and primrose—there are now backhoes and bulldozers and dump trucks. The bulldozers are scraping the land clean. Already they have filled in a livestock pond. Already wildlife has fled. People have seen coyotes crossing busy streets in the middle of the day, found snakes on patios. Mornings, when I run, I scan the sky for the blue heron who used to soar overhead, swooping down to drink from the pond, which is now a mound of dirt. Coyotes, snakes, heron—all of them on the move and looking for refuge.

Often, in the early evening, when I go to our garden to look at the Kentucky Wonders vining and leafing, I imagine my life is sweet and in its proper order. Our rosebushes are still in bloom, the air fragrant with their splendid attar. I check on the blackberry vines we've trained along a trellis of chicken wire stretched along our fence, the wax myrtle that grows at the corner of our house, the lantana with its lacy yellow flowers. We have planted these along with snowball bushes and peonies, marigolds and zinnias, all of which I remember from my father's farm. I watch them grow, and I think back to the way our lot looked when we bought the house—the grass ragged with weeds, the ground splitting open from lack of water, only a few scraggly shrubs along the foundation in front, a gaping wound in the backyard where a satellite dish, anchored in concrete, had been ripped out. Now I fertilize the lawn and mow the grass and weed the flowerbeds, and, when night comes and the gaslight burns with such a warm glow on our front lawn, I think, This is enough.

Then there are other times when I think I'm the most selfish man alive to be here, content, during the season of my mother-in-law's decline.

In "Egypt," Illinois, trappers rig up drowning sets along creeks and streams. They chain a steel trap to a wire stretched taut from a stake on the bank to a sandbag anchored along the bed. Once caught, a muskrat dives and follows the wire into the water. He thinks he's escaping. Instinct tells him he's doing the right thing. But, when he tries to swim back to the surface, his own motion trips a stop-slide L bracket that crimps against the wire and holds him underwater, where he drowns. What he never knows is that, once the trap closed, any direction he moved—up or down—it was all the same.

I imagine my mother-in-law driving the streets of her town in southern Illinois, so far away from us, in a place called "Egypt." It's nearly dark, and she's driving slowly, looking at all the houses where lights are on, where drapes are yet to be drawn. She can see through the windows. She can see sofas and paintings and bookshelves. From time to time she glimpses people: a woman sitting near a lamp reading the evening newspaper, a man home from work lifting his arms above his head to stretch his back, a child running through an archway and disappearing into another room.

The one time she visited us in Texas, my mother-in-law walked through our house, slowly taking in each room. "This is all yours?" she finally said, delight and awe mingling in her voice. "Oh, I'm so happy for both of you."

Now in my dream of her, she keeps driving past the lighted

houses, leaving the people there to go on with their lives, understanding, somewhere in a place more deeply etched than memory, that these houses aren't hers, that she lives alone and has some distance yet to go.

I have no idea whether the Caddo maple in our front yard will survive and leaf out next spring nor how long it will take for my mother-in-law's illness to progress. In the final stage of Alzheimer's, which may take over fifteen years to develop and another seven years to complete itself, the brain's cerebellum eventually ceases to function. The patient loses motor skills, is unable to walk, to sit upright, and exists in a grim twilight in which whatever spirit that remains is trapped in a body barely alive.

I think of winter, of lakes and rivers freezing. I imagine mink, muskrats, otters, hibernating below the surface, dark animals curled asleep in those pockets of air between water and ice. I remember a story I read about the horrible southern Illinois winter of 1830–31. One afternoon the temperatures dropped so severely that a woman, slogging through mud to fetch water from a well, suddenly found the ground frozen around her feet, and there she was, unable to move. She must have been drawing the water, thinking how cold it was getting, imagining the warmth of the fire back at her cabin, not knowing she would soon try to take a step and find herself caught, mud frozen around her ankles. How long did she stand there, freezing to death? The rest of her family had gone to town. The thin trail of smoke from her chimney faded away to a ghostly wisp as the fire went cold, and the only sounds left were the rattle of sleet and the bare tree branches, coated with ice, clacking together in the wind.

Somniloquy

Here's a story that starts one evening when the fire alarms in the hallways of my mother-in-law's assisted living facility let out their shrieks. Inside her apartment my mother-in-law, Wilma, says, "My word." She covers her ears with her hands. "Debra," she says to my wife. "What in the world?"

"It's the fire alarm," Deb tells her.

"Oh, dear." Wilma, who's always been an anxious woman, shakes her head. "Whatever will we do?"

We're staying with her a few days here in Illinois, visiting from Ohio. Because she has Alzheimer's, she tends to ask us the same questions over and over—*Now where is it you live? How many children do you have? Have I showed you this angel someone gave me?* We live in Ohio, we tell her. We have no children. Yes, we've seen her new angel figurine. We do our best to stay patient, to answer her questions as if we're doing so for the first time. After a while, though, the repetition wears on us, and sometimes our voices flatten out or even—yes, we'll later feel guilty—become sharp. A sustained, linear conversation is impossible; Wilma keeps circling back to the same questions, or else she jumps to something that suddenly demands her attention. It might be a stain on the carpet (*Debra, what is that?*) or something far, far in the past (*I had a brother named Paul Hershel, who died when he was a baby*) or something that never happened (*Right after my husband died—it must have been two or three days—a man called and asked me for a date*).

A few years ago Deb went through a time when she'd start talking in the middle of the night. I'd wake to the sound of her voice, and I'd know that she was in some twilight dream state in which she had language but not logic. When I tried to question her, she got frustrated because she couldn't make herself understood. She couldn't communicate what she so clearly knew.

"He won't come in the house," she said once.

"Who won't?" I asked.

"Him."

"Who?"

The more I questioned her, the angrier she became. "Oh, you know."

"No, I don't."

"You know, and you're just being difficult."

"How am *I* being the difficult one? Wake up. You need to wake up."

"I am awake."

"Then tell me what you're talking about."

"Him. He won't come in the house."

Trying to carry on a conversation with Wilma is hard work like that. Occasionally, we can get her interested in a television program, and Deb and I for a half-hour or more can pretend that we're just like any family enjoying an evening together.

Tonight the cable television is on the fritz, and Wilma, restless as she often is in the evening ("Sundowning," the Alzheimer's experts call this increased nighttime agitation), has been picking up her stuffed rooster, the one that crows when she presses on its breast, and asking us whether we've heard it. She's set that rooster to cockle-doodle-doing, only to say again, a short time later, "Have you heard this rooster crow?" She also has a stuffed skunk that wags its tail and plays that Four Tops tune "I Can't Help Myself / Sugar Pie Honey Bunch."

I'm facing an evening of the rooster and the skunk and Wilma pacing her apartment. She's in the intermediate stage of her Alzheimer's now, where sometimes she forgets her children, can't recall her dead husband's name, imagines that her apartment is someone else's home. It saddens us to see her memory dwindling—whole pieces of her life can escape her—but still there are times when the Alzheimer's leads to absurd and puzzling behaviors that amuse us. We try our best to embrace the humor alongside the heartache.

For a while now she's been obsessed with the way she disposes of trash. On this night, just before the fire alarms began screaming, she ate an ice cream bar and then worried about the best way to get rid of the wooden stick that was left. First she washed off the slight smear of chocolate left on it. Then she dried it, wrapped it in a paper towel, and wound masking tape around it. "No one will see it," she said. She carried her little trash mummy to the pail in her kitchenette. There she found an empty milk carton, and she poked the trash mummy into it and said, "Looky here, Debra." She gave the carton a shake. "I put it in this milk carton. It was right here in the trash." She raised her eyes to the ceiling. "Thank you, dear Lord."

She often thanks the dear Lord for small blessings that seem monumental to her: this milk carton found at just the right time, her reading glasses mislaid and then reclaimed, a package of cookies discovered in her cupboard. She gives thanks because she's ladened with paranoia—afraid of the least noise, the slightest movement—and she likes to believe there's a divine presence looking out for her.

Now, mixed in with the fire alarms' screech, I hear people's voices in the hall. If anyone were to ask me, I'd have to admit that I'm up for a little adventure, not that I'd wish a fire, but, still, I can't help being thankful for the diversion that rescues me, at least for a while, from the rooster and the skunk and the trash mummies.

"We better see what's happening," I say.

"Come on, Mother," Deb says. "We need to go outside."

"Outside." Wilma is petulant. "Why?"

"I told you." Deb takes her mother's elbow and prepares to usher her out into the hall. "The fire alarm."

"What in the Sam Pete?" Wilma says. "Cripes. I was going to eat an ice cream bar."

Before her illness she was a loud, brassy woman, who, by god, wanted and usually got her way. I can still hear her carping at my father-in-law, barking his name when she wanted him to step to and do a chore for her: *Loren, Loren.* He was a quiet, fun-loving man who might have had a happier life if he hadn't been prone to fits of depression. He was a mail carrier who wanted to go south, where it was warmer and he wouldn't have to spend the winters slogging his route through the cold and snow and ice. He had a chance to move to Mississippi once where his sister was a rural carrier, but Wilma wouldn't hear of it. "No, no, no," she said, afraid to leave the place she'd always known as home. "I'll never see my mom and dad again." She put her foot down, and that was the end of Mississippi.

I want to be fair to her. I want to say that she was the young-est of seven children, the one the others picked on. They fright-ened her with their stories, tormented her until she was cower-ing under her covers. I want to tell you about the family photo Deb and I have in our home now, the one in which Wilma, seven or eight years old, stands in front of the clan—all those burly, rough-hewn countrypeople—looking small and fragile, her lips held tightly together as if she can't dare say what's in her heart, her eyes wide with a look of fear. I want to understand that since she was that young girl, teased and silenced, she was determined, once she found she had a voice, to use it, to never let anyone own her or escape her grip.

But there are facts. When my father-in-law built their new house in the country, Wilma insisted there be no locks on the in-ternal doors. By her edict there would be no room where Deb or her brother, Mark, might have the privacy they needed to become the people she didn't want them to be—people who would one day figure out how to escape her. She couldn't even stand to see the bathroom door shut. She'd pound on it and shout to Deb or Mark, "What are you doing in there?" To be so frightened that they might be plotting against her, she must have known, some-where in the private talk she talked to herself, that she made it difficult for people to love her.

Above all there is this fact. When Deb's parents adopted Mark, Wilma took the adoption papers and cut out all references to his birth parents so he would never have the slightest clue to their identity. Years later, when he was a grown man, she said to him, "I didn't really want to adopt you. It was Debra who kept yam-mering for a little brother."

It's complicated, then, the way Deb and I respond to her moth-er's illness. There's all this history to muddy up what should be our unconditional love and sympathy. There's this woman who broke people's hearts all her life—who wouldn't allow her husband what he wanted in Mississippi, who kept her adopted son from knowing anything about his birth parents, who did everything she could to keep Deb and me from getting married.

The point is she was a hateful, selfish woman most of her life, and now that the Alzheimer's has accentuated her natural idiosyncrasies—her paranoia; her obsessive-compulsive behavior; her demanding, self-centered nature (does she long for divine protection because deep down she senses she's put too much bad karma out into the universe?)—it's difficult to parcel out our love, wrapped up as it is in all the old wounds. It's particularly hard for Deb, who loves her mother but who also understood years ago that she would never please her, would never fully have her love in return, would never be the sort of daughter Wilma wanted—dutiful, meek, servile. Deb is often headstrong and has a history of being at cross-purposes with her mother. This fact ensures that the present moments will always be full of the past, and that makes everything more difficult than it would normally be. Resentment gets tangled up with love. That's all I'm saying.

In her confusion Wilma has forgotten how much she used to despise me for taking Deb away from her. Because for the most part I stay on the periphery while Deb and Mark make decisions such as moving Wilma to this assisted living facility, Brookstone Estates, and taking away her car, Wilma suddenly thinks I'm the greatest guy in the world. "I've got a good son-in-law," she says over and over when we visit. "He's always been good to me, and I know I've always treated him good."

I never correct her; I let her think what she thinks.

One night—this was in 1996, three years after Loren died and Wilma sold their house in the country, the one she's now forgotten they ever owned, and moved into town—she said to us, "I want to tell you how much money I have." She said this in a whisper and went on to list her certificates of deposit and the banks that held them—out-of-town banks because she didn't want anyone in her hometown to know her business.

"Mother," Deb said, "why are you whispering?"

It was just the three of us in her new house, and it was winter, the windows and doors shut, and locked of course, the blinds pulled down and taped to the window frames so no sliver of light could get in, the draperies pulled and safety pinned where they overlapped in the middle.

"I don't want anyone to hear us," Wilma said.

Deb laughed. "Who could hear us?"

Wilma glanced nervously at the front door, the picture window. "You never know," she said. "You just never know."

Now her paranoia is so bad that she tapes the slats of the vertical blinds at her patio door together so no one will be able to see into her apartment at Brookstone. She disguises her trash: clean wooden sticks, Starlight Peppermints cellophanes, even tiny price stickers. She wraps and tapes them all so there's not a chance that the girls who empty the pails might see something and know that she's eaten an ice cream bar (*If there's a stick,* she must imagine them thinking, *then there's probably ice cream bars in the freezer*) or enjoyed a peppermint candy (*Hmm, wonder what drawer they're in*) or gotten some new blouses (*Hanging in the closet, I bet, and just my size*). She tries to cover her tracks so no one—no sweet-toothed, stale-breathed, clothes-grubbing anyone—will cabbage onto something and walk off with it. When she bundles up her trash, she puts away the signs of her living; she does what she can to make herself disappear.

In the hallway some of the residents are lingering outside their doors, not very impressed with the fire alarms. A group of women in slippers and robes, already preparing to retire for the evening, aren't anxious to vacate the building. They stand with arms crossed over their chests. One of them, a woman with beautifully coifed silver hair, says, "Oh, there's no fire."

Another woman who wears gold lamé slippers complains about the noise. "I wish they'd turn off that racket."

It's summer, and southern Illinois is in the midst of a heat wave. The asphalt streets turn sticky in the sun. Leaves curl for want of water. The corn plants burn in the field.

"I'm not going outside," the woman with the silver hair says. "It's hot."

Then the aides are moving briskly and efficiently down the hall, knocking on doors, telling us to please move as quickly as we can to the outside of the building. "Ladies," an aide says, "Now."

I smell no smoke, hear no whoosh of flame, but the aide's curt, authoritative voice suggests that we shouldn't assume that this is a drill.

Deb and I begin encouraging the women in their robes to come along with us. The woman with the gold lamé slippers gives in. "Ah, the cable's out anyway," she says.

Wilma looks at the women and says, "Why's everyone going to bed?"

"We're not, Mother," Deb tells her. "We're going outside. There might be a fire."

"A fire?" Wilma narrows her eyes and looks at Deb with suspicion. "Is my door locked?" she asks. "I want my door locked."

"It's locked, Mother."

"All right then. All right." She leans over and whispers to Deb, trying to keep the women from hearing. "You know what's in my freezer?" She mouths the words, trying to make them as silent as possible, but still they're audible. "Ice cream."

She's convinced that, when she's sleeping or down in the dining hall for lunch or supper, the girls who work at Brookstone come into her apartment and "walk off" with pencils, paper towels, bananas, her angel figurines. She doesn't realize that she's hidden these things in places no one would think to look. We've found the television remote control in the bathroom medicine cabinet, her purse in the clothes hamper, the peppermint candies she favors beneath her underwear in the chiffonier she's always called her "chester drawers." She fears that people are set on stealing from her, even though she has nothing of significant monetary value in her apartment. Always a collector of kitsch, she has a bookshelf full of her angel figurines. She has trinkets she wins at bingo games, cheap ceramic knickknacks that she sets on her coffee table. She has that stuffed rooster and skunk. Nothing that anyone would want to steal, but don't try telling her that. She's on the lookout.

"Ice cream," she whispers to Deb, and it's clear, even as the fire alarms continue to blare, she can't imagine anything else in the world as dear.

Outside in the summer heat the Brookstone residents gather in front of the building. The women in their robes and slippers are there; a man with a portable oxygen tank on a wheeled dolly, the clear tube snaking up to his nose; a woman wearing a fleece sweat suit in spite of the heat. Wilma is suddenly fascinated with the field of soybeans stretching out behind us, the green plants calf high. "Debra, look at how pretty that field is. Not a weed anywhere to be found."

An aide is telling us to move back from the building to the far end of the parking lot. "If this was really a fire," she says, "you wouldn't want to be so close."

So there goes that mystery. No fire at all. Simply a drill. Now we're left with something to tell later, this story. The woman with the gold lamé slippers grumbles about having to walk across the parking lot. The woman in the sweat suit says, "Oh, well, a little excitement, what does it hurt?"

Deb and I again encourage the residents to follow us across the parking lot. Aides are there to help.

"We better not be out here too long," the silver-haired woman says. "I'm sleepy."

"Ah, you can sleep when you're dead," the woman in the sweat suit says, and the man with the oxygen tank snorts and says, "Yep, that's right. Then you'll wish you had this night back."

Finally, the front door of the building opens, and a woman in a wheelchair comes out, an aide pushing it.

"There's Mary Lou," Wilma says, and she starts to wave. "Hello, Mary Lou," she calls, and several of the other residents join in. "Hello, Mary Lou. Hello."

Suddenly the evening has turned festive. Now that Mary Lou has joined us, every resident is accounted for, and the Brookstone manager clicks her stopwatch, studies it, and then says in a voice straining to be cheery, "All right. Not bad. Fourteen minutes."

"Fourteen minutes," Wilma says, impressed, not noticing the aides' frowns or the way Deb and I look at each other with raised eyebrows. Wilma doesn't understand what fourteen minutes would mean in the event of an actual fire. In her world time has no sequence; she's left that world to us. "Fourteen minutes," she says again.

The woman in the sweat suit says, "Well, that ain't bad for a bunch of old folks."

Then she claps her hands together, and several of the other residents join in. They stand in the twilight, applauding their slow but steady escape.

When I was a child, I was afraid of the dark. If I woke during the night, I immediately called for my mother, and she came and sat beside my bed until I went back to sleep. No matter how I disturbed her own rest, she was patient and kind. She told me to close my eyes and not to worry. "Just think about what you did today that made you happy," she said. "Just keep your mind on the good things."

I'm ashamed to admit that this went on well past the age when it should have stopped. I was in high school—thirteen, fourteen, fifteen—and still calling for my mother those nights when I lay in the dark overwhelmed with a feeling of dread, the world seeming like an empty and terrifying place. The night, that stretch when time vanished and I had to give myself to the current of my dreamworld, troubled me. If I went to sleep, I thought, I might very well disappear inside all that blackness.

Preachers at the Church of Christ assured me this was so. In those days I was preoccupied with thoughts of the world ending, Jesus come back for the judgment. No man knew the hour. Two would be working in the field, and one would be taken and the other left. Two would be grinding at the mill. Watch, the preachers admonished. Be ready—*for in such an hour as ye think not the Son of man cometh*. If we weren't right with Jesus—if we didn't repent of our sins, be baptized, and rise to a new life—we would be lost. I hadn't repented; I wasn't baptized. I was, however, fascinated with the notion of eternity, of earthly time falling away and our souls existing thereafter in heaven or hell. The preachers stood in the pulpit waving their Bibles, shouting about hell everlasting, the lost cast into the fiery furnace to burn there for eternity. I tried to get my head around the concept of "forever," and in my bed at night I began to believe that time might end—that very night while I was sleeping, it might happen—and my good, kind mother would ascend to heaven, and I would be left behind.

I doubt that I would confess this now if not for Wilma and her illness, which takes her from us a bit at a time. Sometimes, as I'm falling asleep in our home in Ohio, I imagine her, alone in Illinois, perhaps not even knowing it's night. On occasion our telephone rings, waking me, and it's Wilma calling, unaware that it's late, past a decent hour for such a call. In the middle of the conversation she can forget who's on the other end of the line or else imagine that we were the ones who called her. She lives in a world where time fractures and swirls around her like the spinning pieces of glass in a kaleidoscope, and she vanishes in the pinpoint center. At moments like this I remember the years when I couldn't trust my own sleep and the horrible feeling I had that at some moment I didn't yet know time might stop and I would slip away.

Still, as afraid of the dark as I was, I couldn't stop my body from moving through it. I was a sleepwalker from an early age and well into my teens. Once, when we were still living on our farm, my mother found me outside in the yard, walking toward our garden. After that she started putting straight-backed chairs around my bed so, if I tried to get up in the night, I'd bump into the chairs and wake myself.

One night, when I was a teenager (we lived in town then), my mother woke and saw that there was a light on in the rear of the house. She got up to investigate, and there I was in the kitchen, pouring a glass of milk.

"What are you doing?" she asked.

"Having a glass of milk," I told her.

Then I drank the milk and went back to bed, leaving the carton on the counter and the refrigerator door open.

Of course, I was asleep the whole time, and the next morning, when my mother told me this story, I didn't believe her. In fact, I remember being a little irritated, unwilling to accept the fact that my body could move about outside my ability to control it. And I didn't like the idea that someone—even if that someone happened to be my mother, who comforted me when I woke in the night—had watched me at a time when I didn't know that I was on display. What business of hers was it if I wanted that glass of milk?

I also talked in my sleep; apparently, I had a habit of swearing profusely. "Those bees, those goddamn bees," my father claimed I shouted one night. "You must not be living right," he said the next morning, "to have nightmares like that."

Sleep talking, *somniloquy*, occurs often with children who also walk in their sleep and is caused, the sleep experts speculate, by anxiety and stress. Like Wilma, I have a natural inclination to woolgather, and, when I was a teenager, thanks to a still-to-be diagnosed overactive thyroid gland, I spent most of my days jittery and frazzled and prone to feelings of panic. The child of older parents, I lived with the constant fear that before I could become an adult they both might die and leave me an orphan. The Vietnam War was still going on at this time, and I feared that such would still be the case when I got to be draft age, and I'll admit that I was terrified by the prospect of going to war.

I was a worrier extraordinaire; it took very little to set my mind firing, my heart thumping, a feeling of dread and helplessness rising up in my chest. Puberty had brought me a bad case of acne, and I worried that no girl would ever find me attractive. Although I was athletic and relatively handsome (at least I sometimes managed to convince myself that was the case), there was that face full of zits. What girl would ever want to gaze lovingly and longingly at that? I worried about clothes. I stood in front of my dresser mirror combing and re-combing my hair. I tried all sorts of acne remedies, imagining that the Clearasil cream or the Phisohex soap really was helping. I sometimes came close to convincing myself that I had nothing to worry about and that soon I would get my driver's license (if I could pass the test . . . I would pass the test, wouldn't I?), and then I'd ask a girl for a date, and the life I saw teenagers living in *Tiger Beat* magazine and on television shows like *Room 222* and *The Partridge Family* would be mine. We lived in a town of a thousand people, and to go to a movie or a bowling alley or a skating rink or a pizza place—those common date venues—couples had to drive to the larger, neighboring cities: Lawrenceville or Olney or Vincennes. The thought of me doing that was enough to deflate the small optimism I'd managed. How would I navigate the highways and the cities themselves? How would I find the movie theaters and bowling alleys and skating rinks (I didn't even know how to bowl or skate), and how many girls would starve while I drove aimlessly unable to locate a pizza parlor? Why, oh why, hadn't I paid more attention while riding in the car with my parents when we went to these towns?

Not only did I walk and talk in my sleep at this time, I also had a recurring nightmare in which I was driving a car across a bridge without guardrails, the sides open to the air and the river below. Always, in the middle of this bridge, everything went dark, and I had to steer the car, knowing that the slightest mistake could send me plunging down into the water, where I would drown.

One night my mother heard my screams, and, when she came to my room, she found me on my back, turned in my bed so my head was at its foot, my legs in the air, kicking wildly, trying to find the brakes on that car so I could stop it. When she woke me,

I was too embarrassed to tell her about the nightmare for fear that, like my father, she would wonder how deviant I was to create a dreamworld full of such terror.

"A bad dream?" she asked.

"I guess so," I told her. I had kicked the night table by the bed, and the lampshade was askew.

Now I think of Gregor Samsa in Kafka's *The Metamorphosis* transformed into an insect sometime during the night and how come morning, when his mother knocks on his door and asks if everything is all right, he wants to explain it all to her. That's what I felt that night with my mother. I wanted to tell her how afraid I was, but I couldn't find the words.

Nights, when Wilma is alone in her apartment, she tends to roam the hallways of Brookstone. The architects designed the facility in the shape of a rectangle, each side looking out on a landscaped courtyard, the corridor turning at ninety-degree angles so, if someone like Wilma steps from her apartment and doesn't know which way to turn to find the dining room or the lobby or the beauty salon, any direction will take her to her intended destination. "I don't know which way to go," she often says, when Deb and I are visiting and it's time for lunch or dinner. "Either way," Deb tells her. "You'll get there. Just keep walking."

Wilma does laps around the corridor long past the hour when all the other residents are asleep. Sometimes she sees a name that she recognizes on an apartment door, and she stops to visit. She knocks on the door and rousts people from their rest. It could be past midnight, but she doesn't realize that. To her it could be morning or noon or early evening.

No wonder, then, since earlier this summer, when the other residents began to complain and the Brookstone administrators told us we'd have to stop Wilma's late-night disturbances, we've had so much trouble convincing her that she's guilty of the offense. She simply doesn't remember it.

"I might go for a walk," she said when we told her she'd have to stop disturbing the other residents, "and I might stop in to say hello to someone."

"Mother," Deb told her. "You're knocking on people's doors when it's after midnight."

Wilma frowned. "I wouldn't do that," she said, suspicious that we were spinning a lie.

Deb made a sign to put on the inside of her mother's door: DO NOT KNOCK ON PEOPLE'S DOORS AND BOTHER THEM LATE AT NIGHT.

The next time we came to visit, we found a line added to the sign in Wilma's defiant handwriting: "I don't, and never did!" The exclamation point accused us of being daft.

After the fire drill Deb and I and Wilma return to her apartment. Wilma eats another ice cream bar; she washes and wraps the stick before she throws it away. We sit in the living room, and she gets quiet. She sits in silence, and I can tell she's brooding over something, trying her best to get it straight in her mind. These are the moments that unsettle me most, when I can see that for at least an instant she understands that something's wrong. An alarm sounds, and she knows she's losing herself. She might ask, in a small voice that carries the shame she feels over not being able to remember, "Debra, what town are we in?" Sometimes she'll look at a photograph of my father-in-law and say, "Now that's my husband, right?" Or, as she does on this evening, "Debra? Do you know of a man? A man my age. A man who might call me sometime?"

Suddenly she's shy but extremely earnest. She's not just spouting off the way she does about her angel figurines, her ice cream, her rooster and skunk and trash. No, this request is sincere and well considered. It comes from somewhere deep inside her, from some pure, true part of herself that the Alzheimer's has yet to erase. It's as vulnerable as I've seen her since her disease began. Something in the sound of her voice carries me back years and years to the nights when I woke, afraid, and called for my mother; something in Wilma's hushed and desperate plea reminds me of my own, and I feel a flutter in my chest the way I did those nights when I called out in the dark and I waited to see whether my mother would answer.

Now I feel this trembling, a dread for which I have no words. When Wilma asks for a man to keep her company, I feel with a shiver how completely and painfully exposed we all can be. It's as if something has sprung open inside her, no matter how firmly the tangled neurons in her brain have wrapped around themselves and strangled her memory. In this moment, in the dim light of her apartment, all the blinds taped shut, the only sounds are the muffled voices of other residents moving by in the hallway or in the apartment next door.

I wait for Deb to answer, knowing, of course, that there's no hope at all at this time of Wilma's life for the companionship she so desperately wants. If indeed there were a man who might have some sort of interest in her, he'd have to be a man whose memory was as bad as hers, who wouldn't mind those repetitive questions, those obsessive-compulsive wrappings of trash.

"No, Mother," Deb finally says. I refuse to speculate on whether it gives her any pleasure to say this. "I'm sorry," she tells Wilma. "I don't."

Wilma sits in her rocking chair. For a good while she doesn't say anything. Then, finally, she picks up the stuffed rooster. "Have you heard my rooster crow?" she asks, and we tell her no, we haven't. We tell her to play it. Play it, we say, and she does. We sit there listening to that rooster. I can't begin to tell you how many times we listen as the evening goes on. Over and over, that cockle-doodle-do.

I'm nearly fifty years old at this point, but still there are moments—Wilma's plea for companionship is one of them—when I feel the boy I was, the one afraid of the dark, the boy who sometimes walked through it like a zombie, sometimes lay in the dreamworld that should have offered peace and rest. He didn't know that a voice was rising inside him—a scream, raw and bruised. Soon it would split the silence of the night and shake his mother from her sleep. She would wonder who this boy was, this stranger, tormented by something he couldn't say. She would wonder what possessed him and why in the world he was calling out to her.

"I love you," Wilma says to us when we're all getting ready for bed. "I love Lee," she says, "and I love Debra."

We say it. We have to say it. We tell her we love her too. Then we lie down in the dark, thankful for the silence that asks nothing from us but sleep.

Take, Eat

A few times each year my wife and I leave our home in Columbus, Ohio, and make the five-and-a-half-hour drive to visit family in southern Illinois, where we grew up on country cooking. Often we fall into a game in which we recall the foods of our childhoods, foods that for the most part we no longer eat because we've been vegetarians for twenty-five years, and I've been mostly vegan for twenty-three of them.

When we first changed our eating habits, we caused our families no end of bewilderment and in some cases downright anger because we so suddenly and certainly turned our backs on the land of beef. We spoke a foreign tongue—*tofu, tempeh, bulgur*—and left those who thought they knew us to shake their heads and wonder about these aliens in their midst. "How will I ever cook for you?" my mother-in-law said in despair. "I'll never be able to cook for you again."

"Remember pan-fried chopped steak?" I might ask Deb when we tire of listening to music and too much silence and boredom fill the car. Then we're off and running, playing this game of free association.

"And meat loaf with Velveeta cheese melted on the top," she might say.

As the miles go by on Interstate 70—Dayton, Indy, Terre Haute—and finally down Illinois Route 130 from Greenup to Olney, we tick off the dishes we recall.

"And fried ham."

"And pork chops."

"And roast beef."

And away we go, all the way home, letting our memory feast on entrées and side dishes and desserts.

Olney is a town of a little over eight thousand people on the flat plains of southeastern Illinois just off U.S. Route 50, thirty miles west of Vincennes, Indiana. I haven't lived in this part of the world in nearly thirty years, but I still think of it as home. I still imagine that one day, perhaps in retirement, I might come back to stay. It's an odd thought, one Deb can't quite abide, accustomed as she now is to a city of good size, but I have this small-town boy part of me that I can't quite shake—that boy who longs for fewer people, more familiarity, a chance to walk down a small-town street and enter a diner or café, knowing that there are friends waiting for me inside, to sit over food and drink and take comfort from the kinship. "What would we do there?" Deb says when we have this conversation about living in Olney. "For one thing, how would we eat?" Then she asks the question more pointedly: "How would *you* eat?"

I have a number of food allergies: processed sweeteners, corn, milk products, citrus fruits, chocolate, nuts. These sensitivities developed after I gave up smoking twenty-six years ago. Suddenly

I couldn't enjoy cornbread slathered with butter, cold glasses of milk, beer, orange juice, chocolate cake, cheese. Now I'm the dinner party guest every host and hostess dreads. What in God's name can they possibly serve me?

Whenever Deb and I come back to Olney, we end up bringing food with us, knowing that there are few restaurants in town that can accommodate us; on occasion we'll pick and choose from Ty's Buffet or have pasta at the local pizza place, and now a café called Ophelia's Cup has opened for business, a café where you can get not only cappuccinos, espressos, lattes, frappuccinos but also nut burgers and vegan soups and herbal teas, and—Lord-a-mighty, I never thought I'd see the day—cucumber-infused water. For the most part, though, Deb and I do our own cooking at my mother-in-law's apartment. When we have a meal with Deb's brother and his wife, we cook something and take it with us. They don't have a clue how to cook for us.

This is farmland, land of grain and cattle and swine. The countryside, in the heart of summer, is prosperous with fields of golden wheat, straight green rows of soybeans, and cornstalks higher than a man's head. The towns, though—ah, the towns. They've dried up and gone to hell. Oil, the region's other industry, has all but petered out. The small towns are filthy with methamphetamine, the drug cooked up from anhydrous ammonia, Sudafed, brake fluid. Meth houses sometimes explode in the middle of the night because someone cooking anhydrous, a volatile chemical that often gets cantankerous, makes a mistake and the whole shebang goes sky-high with a boom and a flash. In the daylight people can drive by these same houses, many of them with paint-stripped clapboards weathering gray, and see the warning signs: KEEP OUT, NO TRESPASSING, PRIVATE. Spot someone buying Sudafed at the Walmart Supercenter, and you can't help but wonder whether they've really got seasonal allergies or whether they're crank addicts.

The Supercenter sits on Illinois 130 on the north edge of town, with a strip mall to its east: a Hallmark Cards, a Dollar Tree, a Fashion Bug. As is the case in so many small towns, Wal-Mart has dried up the downtown area. Main Street is for the most part a sad-assed lineup of empty storefronts or buildings turned into meeting places for fringe church congregations or political parties and social service organizations. Gone is the Tresslars Five and Dime, where I used to drink root beer floats. Gone is Sherman's Department Store, where I worked one summer as a clerk. Gone is the Janet Shop and the Ball Rexall and Beal's Newsstand. No more Town Talk Restaurant or Gaffner's Jewelry or True Value Hardware. Even the Bradford pear trees, which were always so pretty each spring with their white blossoms, have been cut down so the blackbirds won't have places to roost. That's Olney's downtown now, a place not even the trash birds care to visit.

Lately, though, there have been attempts at renewal: in addition to Ophelia's Cup on Whittle Avenue, an Olney institution on Main Street, feared lost forever, has reopened under new ownership—Hovey's, an old-style 1950s-era diner, home of Big Murt hamburgers, greasy French fries, malted milks, fountain Cokes.

Why is it that Ophelia's Cup doesn't completely satisfy me? I had a wonderful vegan soup there one winter's day—a bean soup that was hearty and delicious, a soup I could have just as easily found at Benevolence, a vegetarian restaurant in the Short North district of Columbus. Ah, there's the rub. A soup I could have found in the city, not one I'd expect to find in Olney, not one I associate with my memories of growing up in southern Illinois. "It's like we're not really in Olney," Deb says each time we go to Ophelia's Cup, and she's right. It's like we've escaped back to the

city, and, though I enjoy it, it's not enough to fill the hunger I
have for my memory of this place, where I first knew family and
community and love.

My mother-in-law lives at Brookstone Estates, an assisted living
facility on East Street. Because she has moved into the intermediate stage of Alzheimer's disease, Wilma often forgets that she's
eaten a meal. She can come back to her apartment after having
supper in Brookstone's communal dining room, and say, "I'm
hungry. What you got good to eat?"

One evening, after she'd eaten her supper, she went for a drive
with Deb and me—a quick trip to Blockbuster's to return a video.
When that chore was done and I started driving back to Brookstone, Wilma piped up from the backseat. "Where we going now?"

"Back to your apartment," Deb told her.

"My apartment?" Wilma said this with dismay.

"That's right, Mother. We're going back to Brookstone Estates."

We drove a little ways in silence. Then Wilma, her voice sharp
with disgust, said, "Well, cripes. I thought we was going out to eat."

My appetite has always been good, and, given free range, I would
no doubt stuff in all the foods I remember from my childhood—
not only the meats but also the cheeses and the candies and the
desserts. Maybe it's lucky, then, that I have the food allergies
that I do. Still, I often find myself wishing that I could eat whatever I want without having to worry about the sinus headaches
and respiratory distress that usually follow anytime I mistakenly
think I can eat something from my forbidden list. This is espe-
cially true when I find myself wistful for certain foods—the "Remember This?" game that Deb and I play on car trips can set off
my yearnings as can glancing at the candy section at the grocery

checkout line or seeing *Unwrapped* on the Food Network, that program about how certain products are made: Twinkies, 3 Musketeers bars, Little Debbie Snack Cakes. Just like that, I'm hungry for candy bars, Snickers and Milky Ways and Zagnuts, or snack cakes, Hostess Cupcakes and Snowballs and Honey Buns, or frozen desserts, Fudgsicles and Popsicles and ice cream drumsticks.

Then there's the Christmas holidays from which I remember the chocolate chip cookies my mother baked and the dishpan cookies and the sugar cookies. My father bought candies at the general store near our farm and toted them home in brown paper sacks: chocolate drops, ribbon candy, peanut clusters, sugar-dusted orange slices. I can conjure up a taste right now for those candies and cookies as I can the divinity and fudge and Mexican wedding cakes and bonbons I encounter each Christmas when Deb and I visit family and friends in Olney and they haul out the goodies and say, when I politely refuse to sample them, "Come on. One won't hurt. Jeezey Pete, it's Christmas."

Times like these I ache for that food. I guess you'd say I get nostalgic. *Nostos*, from the Greek, meaning "return home"; *Algos*, meaning "pain, grief, distress." That's the etymology of the word, but I'm not sure that's sufficient to explain what happens to me when I'm back in southern Illinois, unable to commune fully with the people I know there because I can't eat their foods, can't accept their hospitality. No roast beef for this little piggy. No pecan pie. No milk-whipped mashed potatoes. No oranges or grapefruits or tangerines. Not even those. No, it's more complicated than a sentimental yearning for the past because my longing is counterweighted with the thanksgiving I feel because I've escaped the place I now sometimes desperately want to return to and call mine, that place—oh, I know Deb is right—that would never really be a good place for us to live. Still, I can't help but feel that I left a little boy there—the little boy I once was—and the only way I can get back to him is by making myself part of that culture again. How can I, though, when I can't share the most essential custom of eating the native foods?

My father was a glutton. He gorged himself on anything fried, anything laden with sugar and fat. My father-in-law too. He and Wilma's nephew used to have contests to see who could pack away the most food at a single meal. Whole pies he ate. At one sitting. An entire pie.

I come from a land where a man's appetite is proof of his industry. A good worker has a good hunger. The more he shovels down, the more evidence there is that he's work-brittle, a man who can work as hard as the day is long. And the women? They keep cooking it up, Mister. Platters and platters of food. The greatest compliment you can pay a woman in this place is to eat and eat and eat until you're loosening your belt, unfastening your pants, letting your swollen belly hang free while you groan with a delightful agony and say, "Lord, have mercy. I've done died and gone to heaven."

If there is such a place, I bet my dad and my father-in-law are up there now, clamoring: "Enough of this angel food cake. Bring on the cheeseburgers and some apple pie, and put some ice cream on it. Better yet, just leave the carton. Save yourself a trip."

Understand, then, why it was my idea last year at Christmas to stop at Hovey's one evening. We'd been out to the city park to look at the Christmas light display—Deb and Wilma and I—and on the way back down Main Street I suggested Hovey's.

"Just to see what it's like," I said. "You know, now that it's been redone."

Deb gave me that look she has when she's convinced she already knows the answer. "What do you think it's like?" she asked.

"Right," I said, "but what else do we have to do?" Another evening at Brookstone stretched out before us, an evening in which Wilma would repeatedly tell us that someone was sneaking into her apartment and stealing her angel figurines. She'd ask us if we'd ever heard her stuffed skunk play "I Can't Help Myself" when she pressed on its stomach. We'd listen to that skunk again and again. We'd try to watch a television program or carry on a conversation, but neither would be possible because Wilma would interrupt with the questions she liked to repeat—"Did you ever know my husband?" "Is he still alive?" "Now where do you live?" Or the stories she kept circling back to—"My brother, Everett, brought me this angel." "I've got nine ceramic roosters on top of that cabinet." "When I'm taking a nap, someone comes in here and steals things." I pulled the car into a parking spot in front of Hovey's. "We're just killing time, right?" I said to Deb, and she agreed to go inside.

That wasn't the whole truth, that part about killing time. I wasn't aware of it then, but I am now. Somewhere inside me that evening was the ridiculous belief that I could walk into Hovey's, order anything I wanted from the menu and make myself at home, order a Big Murt and fries and a chocolate shake, and shoot the breeze with the waitress about the holiday basketball tournament at the high school, the Christmas lights at the park, the dark days of winter we'd face together, by golly, in this small, wink-you'll-miss-it town.

Only this town wasn't mine, not anymore. All I had were the memories of eating at Hovey's when I was a kid and at other diners and cafés around southern Illinois. I remembered the cheeseburgers and the hotdogs and the hamburger steak platters and the fish sandwiches and the ham and beans. The sizzle of grease on the grill. All manner of pies and cakes in the glass case, the malteds and milk shakes in their tall glasses. Banana splits, chocolate sundaes, cherry parfaits. The bell ringing on the door when it opened or closed. Customers calling out to one another. "Hot enough for you?" someone might say in summer. In the winter a man might shiver, stomp snow from his boots, and say, "Colder than a well digger's ass out there." And everyone would agree. *Yes, colder than a well digger's ass.* Women untied scarves from hairdos freshly styled, and the exciting scent of Aqua Net hairspray spiced the air. High school kids played the small tabletop jukeboxes. The waitress wrote your order on a small pad. "Just a sec, hon," she said when she cleared the dishes away from your table. "I'll be back with your ticket in a jiff."

Oh, what a bunch of sentimental tripe. Let me say it straight out: there was a part of me that wanted to walk into Hovey's and travel back to the person I once was, a person who could eat anything and not give it a second thought, a person who could feel connected to this place and its people. It wasn't the food I wanted— I can see that now—it was the feeling that I belonged to a group. I remember Sunday dinners when relatives would come to our farmhouse, and my aunts and my mother would put out a spread, and all afternoon, as we lazed under the shade trees in summer, cars would come down our lane, dust rolling out behind them, distant cousins or friends come to visit because it was Sunday and everyone, free from work and chores, had time to lollygag. On Thanksgiving and Christmas and Easter we'd take turns gathering at a relative's house, everyone bringing a covered dish, and we'd be this family, tainted with various tensions as all families are—a set of brothers who hadn't spoken for years, for example—

but at the same time full with the sense that we were a tribe, well fed, fat and sassy, in a place we knew as home.

In Columbus I can go months and months and never walk into a store or a restaurant and run into anyone I know. The servers in the chain restaurants are usually college students picking up extra money, but even after four years in this city I've yet to be waited on by one of my own students. The young men and women who greet us at our table are strangers. They don't even write our orders on a pad; they punch them into a computer. These servers are interchangeable, and I'm sure to them we are too. Just another couple of customers in a long line, none of them regulars because in a city of this size there are just so damned many places to eat, and no one really gets to be a regular at any of them.

But in a town like Olney—in a restaurant like Hovey's or any small-town diner with customers who have their own coffee mugs hanging on pegs behind the counter, who have their regular booths and tables, for Pete's sake—you can see the same people. It can be as close to your mother's kitchen as you can get these days, and that's what I wanted, that sense that I was in the company of people who knew me and who would miss me when I was gone. I wanted to be in a place where home cooking provided communion for the tribe.

"Take, eat," Jesus said, when he broke the bread at the Last Supper. "This is my body." He lifted the cup and blessed it as well and said it represented his blood. He said that whoever should eat the bread and drink the cup should first examine themselves to make sure they are worthy of such spiritual union.

I walked into Hovey's—yes, there was a bell on the door that jingled—unwilling to admit what Deb already knew; I was an imposter.

We sat at a table along the wall, and a waitress, a woman wearing a white uniform dress and a red apron tied around her waist, said she'd be with us "in a sec."

"Why'd we come in here?" Wilma asked.

"We're going to have a snack," Deb said.

The menus were on the table, leaning against the chrome napkin dispenser and anchored by the salt and pepper shakers.

"A snack?" Wilma said.

"Aren't you hungry?" I asked her.

"Oh, maybe a little. They start serving at five o'clock. What time is it now?"

The one thing she always remembers, no matter how faulty her short-term memory becomes, is the fact the Brookstone Estates serves supper at five each evening.

"We're not at Brookstone now," Deb said. "It's seven-thirty, Mother. This is Hovey's. Do you remember eating at Hovey's?"

Wilma looked around the restaurant, which was brightly lit. She was facing the front so she could look out the plate glass windows to the street, where cars were driving through the cold night, exhaust coming from their tailpipes. She could see the heavy front door and the screen door that slapped back against the jamb when a man and woman came inside. The man lifted his hand and waved to two women who were at a table on the other side of the restaurant. The woman with him saw the other two women, and she said, "Well, look who's here." The man wore an orange stocking hat. He took it off and stuffed it into his coat pocket. The woman with him unzipped her parka. She had on a blue sweatshirt with three snowmen dancing across the front and white script that read, "Let It Snow." "Weather man says snow's coming," she said to the two women, who were drinking coffee at their table. Then she and the man went over and sat down with them.

Dishes rattled in the kitchen. The grill hissed. A radio on the counter played Christmas carols. The café air was pungent with the smell of beef frying and hot grease, and it seemed to me then, on that cold night shortly before Christmas, the most wonderful place on earth.

"Hovey's," Wilma said, and she nodded. "I ate lunch here sometimes when I worked at the Weber Medical Clinic just down the street."

"That's right," Deb said, and she looked at me with her eyebrows raised, as is our habit now whenever we want to communicate silently to each other how amazed we are by something Wilma says. We were startled by the fact that she so clearly remembered that she had once been a clerk at the medical clinic, that it had been on Main Street, and that she had sometimes come to Hovey's for lunch.

"They had good chili," she said. "You think I could get some chili?"

"I imagine you could," Deb said. "Let's just see."

She handed me a menu and opened one for herself. I read the list of sandwiches, soups, platters, beverages. The selection was, of course, limited. The Big Murt was there, the hamburger steak, the chili, the fries, the apple pie, the lemon meringue, the coconut cream.

I felt—well, how shall I say this? Like a fool. What had I expected? That my menu would be the "special" menu, the one that listed the Big BOCA veggie patty, the seitan steak, the black bean chili, the baked vegetable sticks, the no-sugar apple crisp, the tofu cheesecake?

The waitress's rubber-soled running shoes squeaked over the checkerboard tile floor as she came to our table, order pad in hand, pen at the ready.

"You folks decided?" she asked.

Deb looked at me again, her eyebrows raised, as if to say, *Okay, Mister. What are you going to do?*

"Chili," I said. "A bowl of chili." I pointed across the table to Wilma. "That's what you want, isn't it? Chili?"

"A bowl of chili," Wilma said. "A big bowl of chili."

Deb ordered French fries, and I knew she was invoking her "Don't Ask, Don't Tell" policy when it came to the question of whether the fries were cooked in animal fat.

Which left me, and all I could say was, "A combination salad."

I'll tell you how that made me feel. Like I did when I was in the second grade and my school took a trip to the amusement park at Santa Claus, Indiana. It was a hot day toward the end of May, and on the two-hour bus trip home we stopped at a small-town diner, and everyone ordered pop—Coca-Colas, Pepsis, Seven-Ups, grape Nehis, in ice-cold bottles. They cost a dime. "I guess I can't have anything," I told the waitress. "Why not, hon?" "'Cause," I told her. "I don't have a dime." She brought me a glass of lukewarm water, and I sat there and drank it while all my friends gulped down their pop.

When I got home, I was parched, and my mother filled an aluminum drinking glass with ice cubes and poured Pepsi Cola into it. I drank it down. I told her the story of not being able to get a pop at the diner because I didn't have a dime. "All I had was this," I said, and I reached into my pocket and pulled out a quarter. "Son," she said, "I think it's time we had a talk about money and change." Then she went on to explain that a quarter was twenty-five cents and told me I could have used it to buy a pop and the waitress would have given me a dime and a nickel back. "You mean I could have had a pop?" My mother assured me it was so, and even today I feel so sad for that boy in the diner, sipping that glass of free water. I still get this ache in my throat when

I think of that kid, too stupid about money—too stupid for his own good—drinking a lousy glass of water like he didn't have . . . well . . . like he didn't have a dime to his name, while everyone around him slugged down those pops.

"That's all you want?" the waitress in Hovey's asked. "A salad?"

I knew what she was thinking. What kind of thing was that for a man to order on a cold winter night when there was steaming chili back there, when there was the, by god, Big Murt ready to do business? A salad? A combination salad? Iceberg lettuce, flimsy radish slices, a single cherry tomato?

I looked her straight in the eye. "And a glass of water," I said.

Such an insignificant night in so many ways. A Tuesday. Pine flocking on the light poles along Main Street lifting and falling with the wind. Snowflakes just starting to flutter down. If I were to stand outside in that cold, as I do now in my imagination, I'd be able to look through the plate glass windows into Hovey's, into all that bright light, and see the woman with the snowmen on her blue sweatshirt toss up her hands and laugh and the man with her laugh so hard he has to hold his stomach and the two women drinking coffee, one of them lifting her mug, so the waitress will see and bring the pot.

But first she carries a tray of food to the table on the other side of the café. Well now, this is all right—those people laughing and drinking coffee and the ones on the other side glad to see that their orders have come. What a place to be, out of the cold and with all the food and drink they could ever need. But what's really happening at that table with the chili and the fries and the salad is this: Wilma eats a few bites of her chili. Then she makes a face like she's just tasted the worst thing in the world.

"What's wrong?" Deb asks her.

"I don't like it," she says. "That's not the way I remember it."

She pushes the bowl toward the center of the table. "Here," she says. "You and Lee help me eat it."

"We can't," Deb says. "It has meat in it."

"Ground-up hamburger," Wilma says, not understanding why this might be a problem. "It's cooked up real good."

"Mother, we don't eat meat."

Wilma draws back her head and studies us with suspicion, trying to make sense of it all. "You don't eat meat?"

"No."

"Well, then what are we doing in here?"

Deb turns to me. She raises her eyebrows and waits for me to respond.

I don't have the answer yet. All I can do is close my eyes and bow my head. If I were outside looking in, I'd think the man was asking grace, saying a small prayer before taking up his fork to eat. Even now, I can imagine all the smells and the tastes and the food inside that café, the food that makes me hungry—starved to death—just to think of it.

Not at This Address

I'm at home in Ohio when the call comes. The year is 1986—
fifteen years before I'll settle in Columbus—and my wife and I
live in Athens, where she's in graduate school. It's Saturday afternoon, late summer, and soon, so I think, I'll be running. I'll
start out easy down the long hill to the railroad tracks, past the
row houses where the miners lived when Athens was a coal town.
Then I'll lean into the rise of the hill toward campus, running
beneath a cloudy sky, rain still dripping from the broad leaves of
the sycamores. I can see the route ahead of me: the green athletic
field, the asphalt path behind the redbrick dormitories, and then
the highway, the hill climbing and climbing, the cupolas and
spires of the Athens Mental Health Center towering above me as
I pass along the rocky wall. Or maybe I'll stay along the river—
the Hocking—follow its graceful curve and marvel, as I always
do, over how, years earlier, a team of engineers moved the river
to alleviate flooding. Moved a river, I'll think, and I'll imagine
again the cuts and angles and drainage it must have taken to redi-

rect the river's flow, what lengths it took to change this landscape forever.

But I never have to choose between hill and river because the phone rings, and it's my uncle in Illinois calling to tell me that my mother's health is declining. "She's slipping," he says, and, though I can hear the apology in the way he says it, his voice rises; he practically shouts. I imagine him in his kitchen, staring out the window at the apple orchard and the field of wheat stubble stretching back to the tree line. He's of the generation who always speaks loudly when making a long-distance call, the event reserved for the extremes of emergency, delirious good fortune, or heart-numbing disaster. I remember listening to people calling someone to the phone, the urgency in their voices, the waving of their arms: "It's long-distance. Hurry. Come quick. It's long-distance."

My mother, my uncle tells me, has lost her wits. A group of neighborhood kids come into her house. They steal from her. Worse yet, she gives them money. Blank checks. She signs checks, and these kids fill in whatever amounts they want. "They're robbing her," he says. "Robbing her blind." He reminds me of the money she's foolishly spent on new doors and windows for her house, an elaborate vacuum cleaner / carpet shampooer, and the magazine subscriptions—Lord knows how many magazines, more magazines than she could ever possibly read.

"I know," I say, "I know." And I say it with shame because for some time I've suspected this change in my mother, but I've been afraid to admit it. It's been easier, separated by this distance of some five hundred miles, to pretend that her life is hers and mine is mine, but now someone else has pointed out what I've lacked the courage to own up to—my mother needs me—and, because I am her only child, and because I love her, I have no choice but to face the facts.

"Can you come home?" my uncle says.
And I tell him, "Yes."

When she was a girl, my mother cared for her grandfather, a Civil
War veteran who spent the last years of his life bedfast. She brought
him medicines, turned him so he wouldn't get bedsores, sat in the
dark room and sang hymns—"Blessed Assurance," "Bringing in
the Sheaves," "Sweet Hour of Prayer"—even though she was tone-
deaf and had no voice for the task. She had five brothers and sisters, but she was the oldest, and it was determined early on that she
would be the one on whom the others would rely. She grew to fit
their expectations. She was good-hearted and meek, earnest and
quick to please. Her features were pleasant, nearly Asian in their
delicacy, but, unlike her sisters, she never learned how to adorn
herself with makeup or jewelry, how to dress stylishly, how to flirt
and make boys notice her. She didn't marry until 1951, when she
was forty-one years old, when she must have given up on ever being a wife or a mother. Her name was Beulah Abigail Read, and
for twenty-three years she had been the old-maid schoolteacher
who had bandaged children's scraped knees, helped them get their
galoshes on, pressed them to her when they cried.

I came to her as a surprise, four years after she married. I watched
her help my father on our farm. She used wrenches, chisels, crow-
bars. She lifted cultivators and corn planters, crawled under com-
bines and tractors, her hands becoming scarred and ugly with cal-
luses, bruises, mashed fingernails, cuts.

"I don't hardly know what to do with myself," she told me after my father died. "All my life I've been taking care of someone."

My wife and I leave Ohio, and, as we drive up Route 33 to Columbus and then across Interstate 70 into Indiana and Illinois,
we discuss our options. Deb lets me name them, only offering an

opinion when I ask for one, even though she herself has a stake in this; she has always loved my mother dearly. "Whatever you think is best," she keeps saying, and I know that, whatever I decide, she'll support me. It's clear to both of us that my mother can't go on living in her house, easy prey for the neighborhood kids. And, since we won't be able to move the kids out of the neighborhood, the only alternative is to move my mother.

The question is where. A nursing home, a managed care facility, a shelter care center, a retirement village—I find none of the titles palatable. All of them accuse me, the son who would abandon his mother to someone else's keeping. "I don't think she needs to be in a home," I say. "She can still take care of herself."

And this is true. During the two weeks we spent with her earlier in the summer, I saw no signs that she was a danger to herself. I didn't fear that she would leave on her gas range and burn down the house or forget to feed herself or wander away from home and not be able to find her way back. She still put out a garden and kept her house clean. She tended her houseplants, worked crossword puzzles, helped with Vacation Bible School at church. So much of her seemed familiar to me: the soft tone of her voice; the laugh that turned so girlish when she was really tickled; the way she tapped her fingers on the arm of her chair, forefinger to pinky and back, as if she were playing piano scales. But there were also the oddities: the water faucets she left running, the Chihuahua dog she kept in the house when she had never wanted a dog in the house before, the tawdry glass figurines she bought for outrageous sums from the neighborhood kids. "They're poor kids," she said. "I just thought I'd help them out."

Now the question is how we can best help her. "She could come to Athens to live," I say. "We could rent her a house, somewhere close to us, so we could look in on her."

192 NOT AT THIS ADDRESS

"She could make friends," Deb says. "We could take her to church."

We drive a few miles in silence, each of us, I suppose, daydreaming this scenario. For my part I'm thinking about how much my mother and I are alike, both of us shy, never eager joiners, always uncomfortable in new situations. I'm imagining how it would feel for her to come to Ohio, where she would know only us, and beyond that how she would have to follow Deb and me when Deb finished graduate school and we moved on to wherever there were opportunities for the two of us.

"We'll move her to Olney," I finally say. Olney is twelve miles from her home in Sumner, and her church is there, many of her friends, a few relatives. "Olney," I say again, and I press down on the accelerator, feeling the surge of the car, letting speed lighten the weight that had settled on me when my uncle called. "We'll be all right," I tell Deb, and I let myself believe that all the way to Illinois, where we check into a motel because it's after midnight and I can't imagine waking my mother and explaining to her why we've come.

On Sunday morning, when we finally walk into her house, I feel like an intruder come there, uninvited. The Chihuahua dog, Cuddles, yips and growls. He nips at my ankles, and I nudge him away with my foot. Finally, he loses interest and hunkers down by my mother's chair, where he can watch us.

The quiet that settles over us then is the stillness I've always associated with this house on Sundays. I remember my father napping, my mother reading the newspaper, while the clock chimed off the hours of the afternoon. I open a window, and a breeze puffs out the curtain liners, moves the leaves of a prayer plant on the dining table. That's when I notice the glass figurines sitting on the table, on top of the television set, on plant stands, in the shadow box on the wall—more figurines than I can count. There are poodles and seals, monkeys and dogs, unicorns and cats—all of them no more than an inch tall, made from spun glass, the slender threads like caramelized sugar. I feel like smashing them all.

Then, on the table I see, written on a lined sheet from a writing tablet, in a little girl's scrawl, the name Heather Pennington, and it enrages me to think that this girl, along with her brothers and sisters, have been spending time in my mother's house, have claimed it. My uncle has told me how sometimes my mother leaves them there alone, how they play the radio so loudly the neighbors complain, how they run in and out, screaming, the screen door slapping against its frame. "Like they own the place," my uncle said, and indeed their signs, like the spoor left by wild animals, are everywhere: a kid's bracelet made from candy beads on a string, a pair of muddy thongs, crayon drawings taped to the refrigerator, their names scrawled in my mother's telephone book on the page reserved for frequently called numbers. It is this, finally, that distresses me most, seeing these names and numbers, one of them, again Heather Pennington, written in my mother's own neat hand, on the same page where she has written my name and number. It seems to me a betrayal, as if my mother is saying, "Heather Pennington is the one I can trust."

In this moment a part of me blames myself for all of this. If I had only stayed close, I could have kept it from happening. I'd had the chance. Only three years earlier Deb and I lived an hour and a half away, in Evansville, Indiana, but I decided I would be a writer and a teacher, and the University of Arkansas accepted me into their MFA program, and, though my father died a week before we were to move to Fayetteville and I almost chucked it all to stay close to my mother, I went, with her blessing, and once

I did it became unlikely that I would ever live close to her again, since the only opportunities in that rural part of Illinois were agricultural or commercial, neither of which interested me because she had given me a love for books and teaching, and, though she hadn't known it then, she had also created the probability that one day I would live a life distant from her.

When she comes home from church and finds us in her house, her eyes open wide, and she smiles. "My, my," she says. "What a surprise."

I can see, in the way her face brightens, that finding us here is the most wonderful thing she might have imagined, and I recall how last fall, in a letter, she told the story of being uptown in front of the drugstore when a group of schoolgirls came skittering by and their bright laughter made her wish she was still a teacher. It must be that, the years and years she spent loving children, that has made it so easy to open her door to Heather Pennington and the others.

The phone rings, and it's my uncle calling to see whether we've arrived. He asks me whether I want him and my aunt to come and help explain to my mother what's happening, and I tell him that I do. It is the first time among many over the next few months when I will rely on the kindness of others.

When my uncle and aunt are finally here, we all sit around the table, and I say to my mother, "Mom, we're worried about you."

"Worried?" she says. She keeps her head bowed over her plate, as if she senses what's afoot and is afraid to look up and catch our eyes, her accusers who will demand she admit her failing. I wonder whether in that moment she wishes us gone from her house. "I don't know why you'd be worried about me," she says. "I'm all right."

On the table there are small dishes of boiled potatoes, steamed broccoli, chopped steak—the meal my mother prepared for herself before leaving for church and then warmed in the oven when she returned, insisting that she could fix something for Deb and me (it would only take a whipstitch), but we declined the offer, too anxious to eat. Now I think of all the meals my mother has eaten alone at this table since my father died. I think of the long evenings spent with the television on even if the programs don't interest her. "Sometimes I just like hearing the voices," she told me once. I think of the moment each morning when she wakes from sleep and hears the quiet of her house and wonders how she will bear it.

"It's those kids," I say, and then I let it all come out. I try to say it as kindly as I can. "Mom, we think it would be better if you didn't live here for a while."

"Not live here?" She still won't look up. "Why, where in the world would I live if I didn't live here?"

"Olney," I say. "We've come to get you a house in Olney."

She looks up then and frowns. "Olney." She lets out a nervous laugh. "Gracious, that seems like a world of trouble just because of these kids."

I'm thinking there wouldn't be any of this trouble if she could only tell those kids no. Say no to the kids, to the door and window salesmen, the ice cream peddlers, the magazine solicitors, the people from church who brought her the Chihuahua dog and insisted he would make good company, to the people I won't discover until I start snooping around in her bank accounts—sellers of supplemental Medicare insurance, cookware, personalized pens, costume jewelry, do-it-yourself books. But my mother has never been good at refusing people, and I realize, with a sudden flush of shame, that I'm another huckster, counting on her to be an easy mark. I've come to sell her on this move to Olney, and I'm hoping she'll easily agree.

"We love you, Mom," I say, and even though I mean this with all my heart, because I find myself caught between the roles of dutiful son and con artist, I'm suddenly suspect, and the words stick in my throat.

"Beulah, they just want what's best for you," my uncle says. "You know that, don't you? You know they're good kids."

"Yes," she says, "I know it."

"So you'll let them help you?"

She's fussing with her paper napkin, twisting it around her finger. She bows her head again, and I think of the way each night she kneels at the side of her bed to say her prayers the way she must have learned as a child. I think of how during the past few years TIA's—the small strokes the doctors say are occurring because of arteriosclerosis—come upon her with the least amount of warning: a tingle in her lip, down her arm, and the world tilts. For a few seconds she loses balance, control of her extremities, sometimes consciousness. Maybe at those moments she feels the same thing she feels during prayer—a giving over, a dispossession, a knowledge that, whatever happens to her, it's beyond her control.

"If that's what you all think I need," she says, and just like that, though I'm not sure she intends to, she announces she will hold us accountable. Tomorrow, when we drive to Olney to look for a house, it will be our show, and, though eventually Deb and I will escape back to Ohio, convinced we have done the only thing we can, the consequences will be ours, not only then but always.

Seven months later the second call comes, and again it's my uncle, and this time his news is even worse. My mother has gone downhill, he says. He wishes he didn't have to tell me any of this, but the truth is she's confused much of the time. She forgets the days, forgets to take her medication, wears her shoes on the wrong feet. The past few days someone has been staying with her—this aunt or that uncle—someone with her around the clock because now, as my uncle says, it's hard to tell what she might do. Just the other night, he tells me, she got muddled and went into the clothes closet and peed on the carpet. It is this detail that unsettles me the most, the idea of my mother, who has always been demure and modest, squatting in the dark closet as if she were some feral creature hiding in the night.

Gone is all the optimism I felt back in August when we rented a house in Olney only a few doors down from my mother's church. What a stroke of luck, I pointed out. And there was a front porch where she could display her plants, where she could sit on pleasant days. I made sure the Senior Center uptown would include her house on their van's route whenever she needed a ride to the center for lunch or recreation. And there were relatives in Olney and members of her church who would take her to the grocery stores, the doctor—take her back to Sumner, even, to see to the garden she had left growing there and the fruit trees. I've taken every step to make her life comfortable and safe. I've opened a joint checking account in our names at an Olney bank, and I've arranged for her social security checks and her teacher's pension to be directly deposited. I've paid her rent and utilities. I've sent her money each month for groceries and incidentals. I've done everything I can to make sure she doesn't have money to squander on whatever it is salespeople and telephone solicitors have to offer. Deb and I have done everything we can to make her life good in a place where she knows people, where people love her, in a place away from those kids who stole from her, and now I wonder how much the stress of the move has contributed to her deterioration. I recall that August afternoon—how late it was, how weary my mother looked—when we stood in the house in

Olney, and I asked her what she thought. "We might as well take this one," she said, the surrender evident in her voice. "I'm tired," she said, "and I want to go home."

This time, when Deb and I make the drive to Illinois, we go to do what we tried to avoid in August, to take my mother to a nursing home. We have talked it through and through, considered the possibilities, cursed ourselves for having lives that don't allow us to be caretakers. How would we manage it? We have neither the time nor the space. We live in a small one-bedroom apartment, and we're both gone so much—Deb in classes and rehearsals, me teaching at a small college. We would have to rent a larger apartment, hire someone to stay with my mother. And within the year we might easily be gone (will be, in fact), moving who knows how many times until one of us finally lands the tenure-track teaching position that will allow us to stay in one place. The number of moves will turn out to be four over a nine-year period: two visiting appointments and a Ph.D. program. Each time I will try to imagine my mother going with us. I'll say to Deb, "She wouldn't have been happy with all this moving around. Look what happened when we moved her to Olney." What I won't say is the truth: If our hearts count for nothing, if logic is our only method, it's easy to say (and I'm sure many of my mother's acquaintances have said exactly this) that we could have made choices that would have allowed us to take care of her. We could have taken her with us again and again and again. Had we determined it, we could have found a way.

In 1968, my mother's last year as a teacher, she had to provide a favorite saying as a caption for her photograph in the school's yearbook. She chose, "Never judge a man until you've walked a mile in his moccasins." I like to think that, even as Deb and I park at my mother's house this evening in March and see her shadow move past the living room drapes, that she understands how difficult this is for all of us. Even in her confusion, I have to believe she senses how hard it is to say what's right. Otherwise, I can't begin to forgive myself.

In her house she sits in her chair and holds a Church of Christ cookbook up to the lamplight. She squints through her glasses. "Beulah, what are you looking at?" my uncle says, and she answers in the patient voice I've grown so used to hearing, "A recipe for a Jell-O salad."

The cookbook is upside down, but she keeps moving her eyes back and forth as if she's reading, and I wonder whether she really thinks she's deciphering words or whether she's become a huckster too, determined to convince us and herself that everything is as it should be.

"Why don't you put that down for a while?" my uncle says. "Lee and Deb are here."

"Well, I know that," my mother says with just the slightest irritation, a vinegar tone most people would miss unless they were the ones who had come to spirit her away from this place.

We sit with her, Deb and I and my uncle and aunt, and we explain that in the morning we'll pack her bags and take her to the Bridgeport Terrace, where she can get the care she needs. There will be people there who will make sure she takes her medicine. She won't have to worry about cooking her meals or washing her dishes or shopping for groceries or cleaning her house—all the chores, I'm thinking as we say them, that the people she will soon join at the nursing home would give their right arms in order to be able to do.

"Won't that be nice?" my aunt says.

My mother doesn't answer. She taps her fingers on the arm of her chair, one finger at a time—pinky to forefinger and back, again and again. Finally, she pushes herself up and goes into her bedroom. When she comes back, she has on her coat, her head scarf.

"Mom, where are you going?" I say.

A package meant for a house up the street has been delivered to my mother by mistake. My uncle has written "Not at this address" on the brown paper wrapping and has said he will put in on the porch for the mailman to take in the morning.

"I'm going to take that package to the right house," my mother says.

All her life, since the days she cared for her grandfather and later saved her teaching salary to buy my uncle a winter coat and then became my father's hands, she has always believed in the golden rule—do unto others—and now a package meant for someone else has come to her, and it's her obligation to see it gets to its rightful owner, an obligation she doesn't mean to neglect.

Her goodness humbles us all.

"Mercy, Beulah," my uncle says. "Don't fret with that now."

"It's dark," Deb says. "You don't want to go walking in the dark."

"Mom," I say, "don't worry. I'll take care of it."

She sits down on the ottoman, and she claps her hands together. The noise startles me. "All right, then," she says, and there is a hard, fierce edge to her voice, so desperate she is to have this one final chance at humanity. "If it doesn't get to where it's supposed to go, I won't be the one to blame."

When I was a child, I was afraid of the dark. My mother would sit by my bed until I fell asleep. She would come whenever I woke and called for her. No matter how many times I called, she always came.

On this night, the last night my mother will ever spend in this house or in any other house of her own, I stay awake in a chair, facing the hallway so I can see her if she comes out of her room.

I listen for the sound of her moving about. I'm afraid of what she might do. What if she confuses the closet for the toilet again? How will I handle that? Or any other bizarre behavior? I'm caught in the middle of wishing time would pass quickly so my watch will end and wanting the night to go on and on so I won't have to face the day and what it will bring us.

I'm glad Deb is with me, dozing on the couch; without her I'm not sure how I would manage any of this. She has laid out my mother's clothing, written "Beulah Martin" with a permanent marker on the tags of dresses and blouses and sweaters, on the waistbands of underpants, the backs of brassieres and slips, on handkerchiefs, inside shoes, on my mother's Bible, her writing tablet, her phone book in case she wants to look up an address or call someone. We will take framed photographs to place on the table by my mother's bed, one of my father and one of Deb and me. We will take knickknacks, familiar objects to make my mother feel at home, most of them souvenirs from trips she made as a young woman— a glass-domed paperweight from Brulatour Courtyard in New Orleans, a cedar box from the Wisconsin Dells, a hand-painted china plate depicting the cherry blossoms in Washington DC. To these, over the next year and a half, as my mother's strokes continue and she sinks deeper into dementia and becomes aphasic, we will add baby toys—a ring of plastic beads filled with water, a set of plastic keys—anything she can press and move with her fingers, which will remain active, their constant dance both frenetic and graceful. Deb and I will sit with her and hold her hands still, and her skin will be warm and smooth, and sometimes tears will leak from her eyes as she babbles, unable to say what rises up inside her, whether it be love or rage.

Tonight she comes into the kitchen nearly every hour, fills a glass with water from the faucet, and stands at the sink while she drinks. Deb has helped her brush and braid her hair, and it hangs down the back of her white gown. Without her glasses she looks frightened, vulnerable. I don't speak to her, afraid that, if she sees me there, watching from the dark, she'll be insulted by my vigil. I allow her the dignity of being able to move about as she wishes. Often she leaves the water running, and, after she has gone back to her room, I go to the sink and turn off the faucet.

Then, toward dawn, she goes into the bathroom and switches on the light. She opens the medicine cabinet, takes out a bottle of nasal spray, and removes the cap. She tips back her head, and, as she holds the bottle above her eye, I call out to her. "Mom, no." I rush to her and gently take the bottle from her hand. "This is nose spray," I tell her. "Is that what you want?"

"I thought it was eye drops," she says.

This is the moment I will carry with me always, not because it justifies my decision to take her to the nursing home ("You see, what a danger she was to herself? What else could I do?") but because it is a moment of decency, perhaps my only moment of redemption in this story.

"No," I say, thankful that I've kept her from squirting the nasal spray into her eye, thankful that for at least this one moment I've saved her, saved me, this mother and son who stand face to face. We stand there still in my memory. I hold us there while the sky begins to lighten and the day, its relentless march of time, waits for us to move.

"Thank you," my mother says, and I am filled, forever, with love and shame.

All Those Fathers That Night

I.

The barber works with wood. In a room behind his shop he cuts and planes, sands and stains, fits tenon to mortise. He knows words like *bevel, dadoe, rabbet.* He uses a router jig, a dovetail jig, a biscuit joiner. He powers up his saws: miter, scroll, table, trim. On slow days like this one in this itty-bitty town—it's the mid-sixties, and the kids are starting to wear their hair long, sometimes going a month or more without coming in for a trim—he makes dining tables, end tables, coffee tables, rocking chairs, chests, dressers, armoires. The room smells of the raw wood, freshly cut: the oak and maple and cedar and pine. It smells of stain and varnish. Sawdust coats his eyebrows, the toes of his cowboy boots. He passes the time between giving haircuts and shaves, making furniture for his four daughters, who will one day marry and set up housekeeping of their own. With each cut, each joint, he assembles their futures.

2.

I'm ten years old that day, a country kid, so I won't know anything about the drunk man until later. His story will come to me the way these stories do. Something out of the ordinary happens in a small town and gets told again and again as the years go on until you feel like you were there—right there—when it took place.

Maybe it starts when the drunk man marries, and he and his wife have two daughters and a son. Then, miracle of miracles, his wife delivers triplets, three boys. Just like that, the drunk man doubles his brood.

I wonder how long he basked in his fame—the father of triplets! He must have taken some ribbing, the kind that could lift up a man like him, a man throwing his money at liquor and scraping by on odd jobs and public assistance. Jokes about the lead in his pencil, the pop in his pistol, the twang in his twanger. I wonder how long he got a kick out of that before he started to feel the burden of all those extra mouths to feed.

3.

The state trooper has three beautiful girls. I'll make the youngest my girlfriend one day.

4.

My father only has me, and I was never meant to come along. My parents married late. My father was thirty-eight, my mother forty-one. When he found out she was pregnant, he asked the doctor, "Can you get rid of it?"

5.

Today is my birthday. I sleep late to the sound of rain beating against the windows. The autumn has been cool and damp. My fifty-fourth birthday. I run on the treadmill. I eat a light break-fast. This evening my wife and I will go out for dinner with our next-door neighbors. We have no family of our own. My wife's choice, not mine.

6.

In my dream my father is telling me that there was a time when he nearly left my mother for another woman he swore he loved.

7.

The state trooper, Arky Cessna, comes into the barbershop, mid-afternoon. He's looking for the drunk man, but he doesn't say why.

"Haven't seen him," the barber says.

The barber will always remind me of the television star Andy Griffith. Thick head of wavy hair, disarming grin, good-natured, dependable, upright.

Whenever the barber cuts the state trooper's hair, he jokes with him. "Ark, you better get busy on the fourth if you want to keep up with me," the barber says. "Or maybe these days you're just shooting blanks?"

Ark just nods his head, an agreeable man who doesn't mind a little joke at his expense. By the time I become his youngest daughter's boyfriend, he'll be gone, dead from a heart attack.

I have to admit that I don't even know if he was the state trooper who came looking for the drunk man that afternoon. I just know that it was a trooper, and, whenever I go over the story in my head, as I'm prone to do—it won't let loose of me—I always imagine Ark in that role. I never knew him, never knew the drunk man. They're mysterious figures to me, characters who are just barely out of my reach, disappearing, as they did, right before I came upon the scene. Two men I can't get out of my head, and for that reason alone I set their paths together on this summer day. Ark and the drunk man, one of them looking for the other for some reason I've never known.

So, in my imagination it's Ark Cessna who steps into the barbershop that afternoon, and before he leaves he says to the barber, "Sure is hot."

"I guess it shouldn't surprise us any," the barber says.

Ark laughs and steps out into the afternoon heat.

8.

Summertime. More traffic come evening when folks are off work at the oil refinery, the grain elevator, the gravel pit. Outside the air smells of hot asphalt, cut grass, the fried foods at the café down the street. Inside the barbershop the ceiling fan turns its broad blades in a slow circle, stirring the muggy air. A radio on the counter behind the barber chair plays faint music, the volume turned down so the barber can make small talk with the man in his chair, a man named Red, who works for Marathon Oil. It's after supper, and he has two boys at home, and he's eager to get the haircut done so he can go back to his house and spend some time with his sons.

"Red," the barber says. He hasn't had a soul to tell this to, and he's not even sure he should, but he's been turning it over and over in his head while he worked in the back room cutting lap joints for the drawers of a jewelry chest, and now something makes it a thing he has to say. "Ark Cessna came in this afternoon."

The song the disc jockey on WAKO is playing is Roger Miller's "Chug-a-Lug," a toe-tapper about the liquor that makes *you wanna holler hi-dee-ho*. Red's eyeglasses are folded and tucked inside his shirt pocket. He squints to see who's outside on the sidewalk, a man passing under the candy cane barber pole screwed into the side of the building. "Who broke the law?"

Someone taps on the glass. The drunk man. He's drinking a Pepsi. He raises the bottle, as if to say, *Look here what I'm drinkin'*, and the barber waves at him to come inside. The drunk man just smiles—a goofy, what-the-fuck grin. Then he moves on down the sidewalk toward the post office.

"Who was that?" Red says, and the barber tells him the rest of the story.

9.

My father likes to loaf. He likes to sit in the pool hall, the grain elevator, the barbershop, and shoot the breeze. It could have easily been him in the shop that evening instead of Red because it was summer and we were living on our farm ten miles outside of town, as we did each summer, the school year spent in Oak Forest, Illinois, a southern suburb of Chicago, where my mother taught school for six years until she retired and we moved back downstate to this small town for my high school years.

When I'm a small boy, I have to go with my father to the barbershop to get my hair cut. I can never get comfortable with the way he gets loud in the company of the other men, all of them jazzed up and talking big. They're away from their homes—out of earshot from their wives—and they've got the world on a string. They say things I'm certain they'd never say anywhere but this barbershop, which is a place where they puff out their chests, crack jokes, get rowdy. Sometimes the phone rings, and it's someone's wife looking for them, and, oh, what a howl that sets off, the other men ragging the caller's husband because Mama needs him at home.

I'm a timid boy, more my mother's son, and all the give-and-take between the men in that shop makes me uncomfortable. I try to keep quiet and make myself small. I'm afraid that one of the men might say something to me, might even ask me a question, and then everyone will look at me while I fumble for an answer.

A row of fold-down seats stretches along the wall, and that's where the barber's customers wait or the loafers who've come just to shoot the breeze. They smoke cigarettes and flick their ashes into the silver trays of smoking stands. They drink Pepsis and RC's and 7-Ups from the pop cooler along the front window. They leaf through worn copies of *Police Gazette*. Farmers, mechanics, oil field roughnecks. They roll their short-sleeve shirts tight on their biceps. They keep a cigarette behind an ear or roll a pack in the sleeve of a T-shirt. They handle a Zippo with ease, a casual one-handed operation: a flick of a thumb to open the hinged top; a spin of the thumbwheel against the flint; the flame from the wick touched to the end of a Chesterfield, a Winston, a Marlboro, a Kool; a twist of the wrist to let the hinged top snap shut.

The men tell dirty jokes. They cuss. They argue. They goad each other in a game of one-upmanship. They look for the soft spots, the sores, the sensitive places they know will hurt. They tell each other they're pantywaists, they're pussy-whipped, they're pissing up a rope. From time to time one of them gets another in a headlock and gives him a Dutch rub. They come close to fisticuffs. I know this is the world my father would have me join—a world of cocksure men, a world on the brink of eruption—and, even as a boy, though I can't articulate as much, I must know it's not a world where I'll ever feel at home. I don't even know how to be alone with my father. I always feel uneasy with his gruffness, his quick temper. I never know what might set him off, so I do my best to be quiet, even though I eventually figure out that my silence disappoints him. I'm sure he'd prefer a more spirited boy.

It could have been him instead of Red in the barber's chair that afternoon. I could have been waiting my turn.

10.

On our way to the restaurant we drop off our neighbors' thirteen-year-old daughter at her mother's house. Our neighbors K. and B. married after each of their first marriages ended in divorce. The thirteen-year-old, and another daughter, age twelve, are K.'s. My wife says they're our girls too because we spend so much time looking after them when K. and B. need us to. It's true. They feel like family. I have no siblings, and my wife only has a brother, from whom she's estranged. These girls delight me, and at the same time they make me sad because they remind me of all I never had the chance to experience. They're the ghosts of the children I'll never have.

In the van the conversation is about birthdays. The thirteen-year-old has one coming up in less than a month. "I'll be fourteen," she says, "and then I can date."

She's becoming, B. has told us, boy-crazy.

"Not a chance, missy," B. says. "You're not dating until you're sixteen."

I'm sitting up front with K. He says to me in a low voice, "Well, I guess I've got another couple of years to keep her away from Roman Polanski."

It's a joke about the film director who's been brought back to the United States to face charges of having sex with a thirteen-year-old girl in 1977. I know K. is making light as a way of avoiding the uncomfortable truth: His daughter is becoming a young woman, and all sorts of possible dangers await her.

At her mother's she gets out of the van and stands outside the passenger side door, waving at me. "Happy birthday," she mouths in an exaggerated way. I can't hear the words inside the van. "Happy birthday," she says, and then she runs up the drive to her mother's house.

11.

My father always told me to marry late in life like he did. "Forty," he said. "That's the best time to settle down."

I married when I was nineteen. My wife was a week away from her eighteenth birthday. We'd only known each other four months. Love-drunk kids. No sense at all of what lay ahead. Did we talk about having children? Guess not. Guess I assumed too much. Stupid me.

12.

Inside the shop Red and the barber hear glass breaking against the outside wall. "Kids in the alley making a mess, most likely," the barber says. "I'll jerk a knot in their tails. Be right back."

13.

The triplets are fourteen the evening their father steps into the alley between the post office and barbershop. Does he know Ark Cessna has been looking for him? Does he carry something inside him that makes him crazy-scared on this summer night? By this time his three older children are grown and gone from home. Just a handful of years and the triplets will be too. They'll marry good women, have families, hold down jobs, be upright and honorable men. Flawed as he is, and as often as he's disappointed his family, the drunk man still has this ahead of him: the satisfaction of seeing his darling boys become good men. It's right there, just a few years out ahead of him, the chance to see his own youth reflected back to him, only the way it should have been all along without the liquor—a decent life, nothing to give him shame, and maybe that's what's too much for him to stand, the unavoidable comparison, the accusation, the reminder he gets each time he looks at those boys that time and time again he fell short of being the father his children deserved.

14.

My father never intended to have a child in his middle age, but, as we all know, our nevers sometimes turn into exactly what we swore was impossible.

Once upon a time, maybe ten years back, my wife decided she wanted to have a baby. I would have taken that miracle, a child in the middle of my life. I like to tell myself it wouldn't have thrown me for a loop. Then, she said, she came to her senses, and that maternal feeling, much to her relief, went away.

15.

Fifty-four. My life more than halfway done.

16.

The barber finds the drunk man in the alley, the jagged end of the Pepsi bottle near where his body thrashes about on the ground.

He's slashed his throat, cut his jugular, and now blood spurts from the wound, more blood than the barber knows how to stop with his hands, those hands that work with wood.

Inside the shop Red hears the shouts for help. He runs out of the shop, the cloth, white with thin blue stripes like pillow ticking, still snapped around his throat. The long cloth fills with air and billows around him as he runs.

His older son is ten, and at that moment he's in the backyard, tossing one of those toy parachute men up into the sky. At the zenith the handkerchief-sized parachute unwinds, and the plastic parachute man drifts gracefully to earth.

Just four years from this night my family will move into a small frame house in this town, and Red's son will be one of my friends. I'll hear the story of the drunk man. I'll go to high school for one year with his triplets before they graduate. Three blond-haired, blue-eyed, rugged-looking boys with charming smiles. Darlings in this town.

I have my father's 1930 yearbook, *The Pyramid*, and in the grade school photos there's a picture of the drunk man, who is, I'd say, about ten years old at the time. He looks older, more world-wise than his peers. He has a jaunty cock to his head, a weary look in his eyes. Maybe he's starting to think, even then, The hell with it all.

17.

The barber calls Charlie Sivert at the funeral home. Who else do you call in a town where there's no doctor, no hospital, no ambulance service? You call the man who presides over the dead.

And that's what the drunk man is by the time Charlie arrives. Dead in the alley. Dead despite anything Red or the barber can do to save him. Dead by his own hand. Dead with six children left behind. Dead with those triplets yet to grow into men.

Later, Red's son tosses his parachute man into the sky again, and, while he watches its descent, one of those three boys—it's so hard to know which one—runs beneath it, cutting across the yard to his uncle's house. And like that the news of what happened in that alley begins to be known.

18.

"If *ifs* and *buts* were wishes and nuts," my father always said, "we'd all have a merry Christmas."

19.

The barber has to go home. Red has to go home. They have families waiting. The barber's four girls; Red's son.

The girls wait for their father and the familiar scents he carries with him: Lucky Tiger hair tonic, Butch Wax, Mennen talcum powder—that and the sweet smells of cut wood and varnish. How long will it be before he'll be able to power up a saw, watch the blade slice through wood, without thinking of how he found the drunk man in the alley and how he tried to stanch the blood with his hands?

Red's son holds his parachute man and wonders why that boy has just run across the yard.

I imagine everyone moving now as evening turns to dusk: Charlie Sivert and the barber and Red loading the drunk man's body onto the gurney and into the hearse; the barber and Red washing blood from their hands, the best they can, in the barber's sink. What do they say to each other? How do they step back into their regular lives? When they come into their homes that evening, do they try to tell the story to their wives outside their children's hearing, not wanting them to know the way a misery can fester until a man can give someone a silly grin and a wave and then step into an alley and cut his throat.

The drunk man's brother gets the news and doesn't know what to do with it. Ark Cessna hears the news and doesn't know what to do with it. The drunk man's wife, his children, those triplets. They don't know what to do with it.

Neither do I. I don't know why the law was looking for the drunk man. I don't know whether that was the reason he cut his throat. I could ask questions. The barber is still alive. The triplets still live in that town. I could be forward. I could say, "Was your dad in trouble with the law?"

But it's everything I don't know that keeps me telling the story. As long as I don't know why the drunk man did what he did, I can fit the story to my own—the story of an only child who has no children, an only child born to a father who may have come to love me but at first was willing to let me go.

The story of the drunk man comes to me year after year, and attached to it is the story of Ark Cessna and the daughters he left to mourn him once he was gone. Neither story is mine to tell, outside of the fact that each is a story of fathers and their children.

So here I am, on my fifty-fourth birthday, past any chance I ever had of being a father. I think of how my father asked the doctor if he could "get rid of it." I think of Ark Cessna's beautiful girls and the barber's too. I think of Red and his son, who's still my friend and willing to ask his mother, for my benefit, everything she remembers about the night the drunk man smashed that Pepsi bottle and worked the jagged end into his throat.

All those fathers that night. They must have been afraid, scared to death, for, once the drunk man killed himself and those triplets became the town's to see to, the world, and everything they thought they knew about it, surely seemed flimsy, about to come apart with the slightest breath or step.

And yet there were all those children, and someone had to look over them. Someone had to keep telling them, *Love, love, love*—until, finally, they believed they were safe.

I can't let the story go because there are times like this, another year older, when I wish my father back to me—when I imagine the children I never had, the grandchildren he never had. All of us come together. All of us with all our lives to live—lives of plenty, with nothing to long for and nothing to regret.

In the American Lives series

To order or obtain more information on these or other University of Nebraska Press titles, visit www.nebraskapress.unl.edu.